IELTS **Writing Task 2**

SENTENCE
GUIDE

IELTS PODCAST
with Ben Worthington

Contents

Preface

FREE ESSAY CHECK FOR AMAZON ORDERS.

After studying the Sentence Guide I want you to send me your essay for a FREE ESSAY CHECK.

I want to help you by sharing my knowledge, TIPS and professional advice.

This way you can be sure to pass the exam.

I can check your essay and show you where you went wrong.

I will tell you if you are strong in Lexical Resource, Coherence, or if your essay scores full points for Task Response.

Discover the mistakes you make -so you don't do them on TEST DAY

I want to support, motivate, and push you to pass the exam!

Let me give you valuable feedback showing you the errors that would cost you points. Let me HELP you pass the exam.

Send your essay to me at ben@ieltspodcast.com along with a copy / paste of your Amazon receipt.

This offer is only available within 30 days of buying the Sentence Guide book.

GOOD LUCK!!!!

Introduction

Ben: Hello there. Thanks for buying the sentence guide. I'm just going to give you an overview of the process what we're going to do, how we're going to do it, and why? **This pack expires in a month** because I want you to move fast. If we don't have deadlines, things just linger, they carry on, we don't get through the project, we don't get through the work. You have around 31 days from the purchase date. Just to bear in mind.

I'll be as quick as possible giving you your answers back. This way, everybody moves faster, and we get closer to the goal of passing IELTS, getting the immigration papers, getting into university, getting a seven, eight, or nine, just moving on and leaving it all behind us.

The first few chapters, we're going to look at the building blocks. We're going to look at building a solid foundation for the essay. That means starting perfectly, getting in the correct ideas.

We will look at how to classify an essay, the basic structure, the paragraphs, and then the sentences within the paragraph.

There are two words of warning that I want you to pay attention to. Firstly, in the essay checks **I won't check your spelling.** The reason is because we have computers that can do this for you. I can spend more time telling you about coherence, correcting third person singular mistakes etc.

Even before doing any essay writing get into the habit of checking your own spelling and grammar. If you do have a problem, I'd recommend sorting it out first, because that is going to definitely lose you marks. There's no amount of essay checking I can do that will help you.

Identify all the words that you spell wrong, make a list, go into Google, put "online spelling test". Go there. Every day, start testing yourself on how to do the spellings. Get your spelling under control.

I cannot learn English for you. I can teach you English, but I cannot learn it for you. This means that if you do have the spelling mistakes, it's up to you to do the work.

If you do have challenges with the use of articles or third person singular, **I can identify and show you,** and even send you specific exercises, **but it's still going to take a lot of work from your side.**

Have a listen to chapter one, if you have any suggestions send them to me.

1 Concept of an essay and Marking Criteria

There are essential points that you need to bear in mind when you are writing an essay, especially an IELTS essay. You are graded based on the following criteria:

- ## Task Response

You satisfy the Task Response when you answer the question being asked. You do this by **fully addressing all the parts of the task**. You need to present a fully developed stance when you answer the question by **elaborating ideas clearly** and **justifying these with convincing arguments.** It is important to be direct to the point and avoid beating around the bush. Most people do this without realizing that they are already **deviating from the question,** so it's really important to analyse the question correctly.

- ## Cohesion and Coherence

Ideas and information should be linked together in a **logical and organised** manner in order to score high on Cohesion and Coherence. There should be a **central topic in each paragraph** and a clear progression of thought throughout the essay with a **smooth transition of ideas** using effective paragraphing, sentence structures and other transition devices.

- ## Lexical Resource

Lexical Resource is your **range of vocabulary.** You have to show **flexibility** and **precision** in the words that you use. You do this by varying your words and using accurate synonyms instead of

repeating the words to describe something over and over again. **Can you say, "Jobs" in three different ways, but using different words?** For example, employment, position, posts, responsibilities, those kinds of words -- different words to describe similar things.

- ## Grammatical Range and Accuracy

Finally, you have your Grammatical Range and Accuracy that measures your prowess in grammar. This would cover your subject-verb agreement; consistency of tenses; the appropriate use of articles, prepositions and conjunctions; and variation in sentence structures.

Language vs. Reason

What's really important about these four criteria is that absolutely **none of them ask about the quality of your ideas, so do not worry if you're writing basic ideas.** Do not worry about writing amazingly intelligent answers. The quality of the idea is secondary. What the IELTS test stands for is, International English Language Testing System. It doesn't want to know about your ideas or their quality. If it asks you about pollution, it doesn't really matter if you can describe an engine or not, or about the CO2 and stuff. It **only pays attention on what vocabulary you're going to use.**

Though the quality of the idea may be secondary, it has to be realistic, but it doesn't have to be anything amazing, because the examiner's not going to pay much attention. They will look for mistakes, readability and other factors. He's going to be using the criteria we just mentioned, so bear that in mind.

1.2 Paragraphs built around ideas.

The writing part is about organization, basically four paragraphs. This is the model I teach. You have an introduction, paragraph one, paragraph two, conclusion. **The main points where you score -- are in your body paragraphs.**

The fundamental point to build this **body paragraph** is having an idea, a position or an opinion. You need this idea. To get the idea, you need to be skilled in reading the question, analysing the question and then producing an idea. Once we have the idea, we can build the paragraphs. Then, once we've built the paragraphs, the introduction's easy and the conclusion's easy.

Once we can get these two ideas -- one idea for paragraph one, one idea for paragraph two -- then **from these two ideas we can build a full paragraph** -- write down the four sentences roughly. Then, we can do the conclusion and then the introduction, or the introduction and then the conclusion. **It is fundamental to have one simple idea.** It doesn't even have to be amazingly sophisticated; there has to be one believable, logical idea. Then,

we build an essay around it. We build a paragraph around idea one, we build another paragraph around idea two. But first and foremost, we will look for two ideas.

2 How to get ideas for your essay

After receiving the question sheet from the invigilator, you need to read the question thoroughly and you must try to understand what it says and what it requires you to answer.

Once you have read and analysed the question, you need to figure out how you will answer and how you would go about developing these answers.

> **You have to choose carefully which ideas you should include in your essay and which you should simply ignore.**

All concepts must move to satisfy the question and progress to elaborate these concepts without deviating from the main topic.

But how do you formulate your ideas?

> Try to get used to seeing a question and extracting two <u>basic</u> ideas with <u>examples</u> for paragraphs.
>
> These points are your paragraphs.
>
> Once you have your two simple ideas / <u>sentences</u> (P1 and P2) the whole essay starts.
>
> VIDEO: **Essay Topics with Answers**

Depending on the question, our ideas will be different.

1) Opinion
These questions ask you your opinion, you can be totally against or totally in favour. You give two reasons, (one in each paragraph), and write your opinion in the introduction and conclusion.

The internet has had a significant influence on the culture of many societies. To what extent would you say that the internet has positively or negatively affected the development of your society?

P1 positively 100% reason 1 +example
P2 positively 100% reason 2 +example

2) Discuss + Opinion

This means you consider both sides of the question, a paragraph for each. If your **personal opinion** is required, put it in the introduction and conclusion.

The idea of having one job is becoming old fashioned. The new fashion is to have several jobs or ways of earning money. To what extent do you agree or disagree?

Can you see how we have two views here?
Then a 'to what extent do YOU AGREE / DISAGREE'   this is confusing

When making my plan I'm just going for a simple coherent which is easy to understand and explain...

P1: AGREE one job is old fashioned ..... +example

P2: AGREE several jobs the norm .....+example

To conclude my opinion totally in favour of modern new trend of 'career hopping'

3) Problem + Solution

This isn't difficult. For the first paragraph discuss the problem, for the second paragraph give the answer.

Because of new subjects such as computer programming studies, numerous education centres have dropped music   from the curriculum. How important is music in a young person's education?

P1 Schools dropping music. Explain why......+example
P2 Music is important for children because....+example

4) Two Part Question
In western universities there are severe problems with students and their behaviour. What do you think are the causes of this? What solutions can you suggest?

Easy. One paragraph for each question.

P1 Causes of bad behaviour? Explain why......+example
P2 Solutions....? +example

ACTION 1

Read through ALL of these questions, and try to determine a P1 and P2.

Discuss + Opinion

1. It is thought that using leisure time for activities to improve the mind, such as reading and doing word puzzles, is important. Other people feel that it is essential to have a rest and relax during leisure time. Discuss both views and give your opinion.

P1:
P2:
Opinion:

2. Some people say that universities should be concerned with educating people so that they will have more general knowledge and be able to consider important matters from an informed viewpoint. **Other** people say that universities should simply train students to do the jobs required by society and not concern themselves with broader issues. Discuss.

P1:
P2:
Opinion:

3. Some people said the age of books is past. Information will be presented by video, computers, televisions, films. **Others** think the books and written words will be necessary for spreading information and completing education. Discuss.

10

4. Going abroad for higher education is an expensive prospect for many people, possibly with some disadvantages, it is probably better to go because of the new culture and language found studying in a different country. To what extent do you agree or disagree?

Opinion

5. Studying a local language in the host country is the ideal **but** not the only way to learn the language. Do you agree with this statement?

6. The internet is dangerous because it has destroyed communication between friends and family. Some people say that it steals time from real life interactions. To what extent do you agree or disagree?

7. Subjects such as Art, Sport and Music are being dropped from the school curriculum for subjects such as Information Technology. Many people believe children suffer as a result of these changes. To what extent would you support or reject the idea of moving these subjects from school curriculum?

8. It has been claimed that workers over 60 are not responsive to rapidly changing ideas in the modern workplace, hence the preference for younger workers. To what extent do you agree or disagree?

P1:
P2:

Problem + solution

9. People in all modern societies use alcohol, but today's youth are experimenting with both binge drinking and social drinking. Some sociologists claim that parents and other members of society often set a bad example. Discuss the causes and some effects of widespread alcohol abuse by young people in modern day society. Make any recommendations you feel are necessary to help fight excessive drinking.

P1:
P2:

10. We can get knowledge from news, but some people think we cannot trust the journalist. Discuss, what you think are important qualities a journalist should have?

P1:
P2:

11. News editors decide what to broadcast on television and what to print in newspapers. What factors do you think influence these decisions? Do we become used to bad news? Would it be better if more good news was reported? Discuss.

P1:
P2:

12. In some countries the average worker is obliged to retire at the age of 50, while in others people can work until they are 65 or 70. Meanwhile, we see some politicians enjoying power well into their eighties. Clearly, there is little agreement on an appropriate retirement age. Until what age do you think people should be encouraged to remain in paid employment?

Two part question

13. We have been living in the nuclear age now for over half a century. Since the first atomic bombs were developed, nuclear technology has provided governments with the ability to totally destroy the planet. Yet the technology has been put to positive use as an energy source and in certain areas of medicine. To what extent is nuclear technology a danger to life on Earth? What are the benefits and risks associated with its use?

P1:
P2:

14. Some employers reward members of staff for their exceptional contribution to the company by giving them extra money. This practice can act as an incentive for some but may also have a negative impact on others. To what extent is this style of management effective? Are there better ways of encouraging employees to work hard?

P1:
P2:

15. Most of the world's poor live in countries where tourism is a growing industry. The issue is that tourism does not benefit the poorest. How can the income generated by tourism benefit the poor? And how can we ensure that tourism does not destroy traditional cultures and ways of life? Discuss.
P1:
P2:

16. Over the past fifty years, young people began to gain status and power lost by old people. What is the cause and is it a good development or bad?
P1:
P2:

POSSIBLE EXAMPLE ANSWERS
Also search for this video:

IELTSPodcast Essay Topics with Answers

Discuss + opinion

1. Some people think that it is important to use leisure time for activities that improve the mind, such as reading and doing word puzzles. **Other** people feel that it is important to rest the mind during leisure time. **Discuss both views and give your opinion.**

P1: Improve the mind stimulus, make use of idle time, possibly even learn or improve a language with new apps
P2: Important to rest the mind .... because can be stressful at work, better performance at work ....
To conclude it depends on the line of work / job you have, if you are tired then relax if not then you should make use of the time.

2. Some people say that universities should be concerned with educating people so that they will have more general knowledge and be able to consider important matters from an informed viewpoint. **Other** people say that universities should simply train students to do the jobs required by society and not concern themselves with broader issues. Discuss.

P1: More valuable workers, better informed etc EG General studies...
P2: workers more practical more valuable to society.... and they finish with debts and need to a job ...quickly
Conclusion, I believe should be taught practical skills for paying off debt

3. Some people said the age of books is past. The information will be presented by video, computers, televisions, films. **Others** think the books and written words will be necessary for spreading information and completing education. Discusss.

P1: books are past... sales at Amazon kindle,,, etc...
P2: spreading info, newspapers, in poorer parts of the world.... etc...

Conclusion, my opinion, eventually as electronics fall in price, and countries slowly increase there earnings paper will eventually be less common...

4. Going overseas for university is an expensive prospect for many people. **But** while it may have some disadvantages, it is probably better to go because of the new culture and language found studying in a different culture. To what extent do you agree or disagree?

P1 Is expensive, currency, accommodation, start up costs...
P2 advantages of going abroad are new culture, language... job prospects...
To conclude, more expensive going abroad but should be seen as an investment not a cost...

Opinion

5. Studying a local language in the host country is the ideal **but** not the only way to learn the language. Do you agree with this statement?

P1 I agree is the best because ...
P2 I agree not the only way because

3 How to build the paragraph around the idea

We can follow an acronym for the whole essay. This way we know EXACTLY what to write and where.

GOT   FWEgT   SWEgT   C-It

INTRODUCTION = GOT

G = Sentence 1 = S1: This general sentence introduces the essay.

O = S2: Here I place my opinion and my main reason (sometimes you may need a second sentence to describe P2).

T = TS3: Here is a universal sentence you can place if you have problems writing the stated amount of words:

This essay will discuss both sides / issues, using examples to demonstrate points and support arguments.

PARAGRAPH 1 = FWEgT

Fp1 = *FS4: Firstly, Your position (P1).*

W = *WS5: Why? Why do you think this? Explain your position, 'This is largely because...'*

Eg = *EgS6: For example.... Give a real life example that proves your case.*

T = *TS7: Therefore....   This sentence links your argument back the main idea P1.*

PARAGRAPH 2 = SWEgT

Sp2 = *SS8: Secondly, Your position (P2).*

W = *WS9: Why? Why do you think this? Explain your position,*

'This is largely because...'

Eg = *EgS10: For example.... Give a real life example that proves your case.*

T = *TS11: Thus.... This sentence links your argument back the main idea P2.*

CONCLUSION = CIt

C = *CS12: C*   **To conclude from the examples and arguments given I firmly believe / disagree that** _____

It = *ItS13:* **Optional** *sentence to show the other side of the opinion. If possible use the 'It is...' structure.*

> Now we are familiar with the structure to follow, lets have a look at it in action in the next chapter.

3.1 Power Essay Challenge 1

The next task will give you an intense exposure to native style writing and collocations. Soon you will start incorporating these new grammar structures and collocations into your own writing.

When you have done it, send it to me and I'll have a look.

All the instructions are in the audio mp3 on the page below.

Do number 1 to start with.

IELTS Power Essay Challenge 1

http://www.ieltspodcast.com/ielts-power-essay-challenge/

3.2 The Fastest Grammar Lesson Ever.

Universal Sentence 1:

THE ISSUE OF __(ISSUE)_ HAS GROWN IN IMPORTANCE

___(TIME FRAME)____.

The issue of poverty in developing countries has grown in impor-tance *over the past few decades.*

has grown in importance *year on year*

since _____the beginning of time

Universal sentence 2

This is due to the fact that

For example recent (IMF, governmental, council) studies show that 6.7% of .....

UNIVERSAL STRUCTURE 3

Whether advertising innocently informs or misleads the masses has been debatable since its inception around the industrial revolution.

Whether pollution is a price to pay for prosperity or a dangerous by-product of a senseless capitalistic system is a debatable topic, especially in the West.

Whether public education is a problem or opportunity for the government is a sensitive issue that needs to be analysed in a careful manner.

Whether universities should charge for access or be open to the public is a sensitive issue concerning many stakeholders and therefore should be analysed carefully.

The issue of whether universities should allow free access or charge has grown in importance over the last few decades.

The issue of whether international students should be allowed access through merit or money has grown in importance over the years.

A VERY EASY STRUCTURE TO INCORPORATE
It should be FIXED,

IT + MODAL + BE + Past form = Points!!!
It should be INTRODUCED
It should be FORGOT
It must be NEGLECTED
Transform these:
It must be LEAVE -
It should be DEAL -
It cannot be SAY -
It should be TAKE INTO ACCOUNT -

CONDITIONAL

Therefore it is clear that if the internet continues gaining in popularity there would be more positive implications.

Therefore if schools continue to rely on getting knowledge from corporations there could be serious implications.

CONDITIONAL

Pick up some points by using this conditional sentence to extend your arguments in the body paragraphs.

IF _____ did happen / were introduced / were implemented, there **WOULD** be at least two / three major consequences. Firstly.... Secondly....

EXAMPLES:

If governments **increased** spending on education, students **would see** the following benefits: Firstly.... Secondly....

If equality legislation **were introduced** globally, the effects **would** most likely be felt in the following ways. Firstly....Secondly....

If _____ did happen / were introduced / were implemented, there **would** be at least two / three major consequences. Firstly.... Secondly....

the main two consequences **would** be:

CONCLUSION

Although ACID RAIN / ADULT EDUCATION / PUBLIC SCHOOLS are unjustifiably _____ they are ARE STILL ...(BENEFITS)..TO BE GAINED

Although public education is unjustifiably the ideal solution they are ARE STILL ...(BENEFITS)..TO BE GAINED with a private education sector.

Although war appears inevitable, fortunately there are ARE STILL people actively involved in organisations to prevent it.

3.3. Power Essay Challenge 2

All the instructions are in the audio mp3 on the page below.

Do number 2.

4 Essay Checking Tip

Now that you've got your essay in front of you, have a look at it, and make a list of those mistakes that you've made.

From past experience I know the main problem areas are often:

-Third person singular
-Tense agreement
-Singular plural agreements
-Articles

Have a look at your essay and make a list of the errors, usually the you will know the theory and just forgot to apply it, in other cases you have to study. See below for some useful links.

You need to get these errors under control, or you will loose points.

If you're working to a tight deadline, if you have your exam in two or three weeks, maybe you don't have time to study these grammar points. What you need to do is memorize this list so as to remember where you make your errors. **Memorize the list.**

Then every time you finish a piece of writing, you go back to your memorized error list, and you say, "In that last test I wrote, I made a mistake with the tense agreement. So now, five minutes before the exam finishes, I am going to look through my essay. I am going to go through very, very, very, very slowly, with lots of concentration, and look for the mistakes that I made in my last essay. Because more than likely, I have probably made them again in the next essay, especially, if I didn't have time to really study them."

Work through correcting the errors. **You are correcting the essay so the examiner doesn't have to**. This way, you'll increase your exam results by around 10 percent, especially if you do it well. You're seeing the problem before the examiner does.
You are going to score a lot higher if you're self correcting your essays.

Here are some links to help you study the mistakes you have made.

ARTICLES
British Council – Determiners and quantifiers.
Toronto University – Excellent explanation.
English Grammar in Use – full textbook. Great resource.
English in Use – Online quiz to test your knowledge.

PREPOSITIONS
Georges Online – Fantastic little test maker, try copy pasting articles you read normally – to make it more interesting.

Online Prepositions test
Explanations 1
Explanations 2
Explanations 3

In the next chapter we're going to look at more complex sentence structures, and writing more sophisticated essays. Have a listen to the next chapter, and remember to send me an email with your thoughts, suggestions, ideas, improvements.

5 Yet, However, On the one hand...

DISCUSSION + OPINION

Y OT	Fp1 W eg T	Sp2 W Eg T	C It

Here is a guide to what you should write for each sentence. To use this effectively you must have P1 and P2 ABSOLUTELY clear.

P1 and P2 depends on the essay but will usually be your opinion, or your problem to discuss.

INTRODUCTION

Y = *Sentence 1 = S1: This general sentence introduces the essay and uses a more advanced structure 'yet'.*

O = *S2: Here I place my opinion and my main reason. Sometimes you may need a second sentence to describe P2.*

T = *TS3: Here is a universal sentence you can place if you have problems writing the stated amount of words:* **This essay will discuss both sides / issues, using examples to demonstrate points and support arguments.**

A company has announced that it wishes to build a large factory near your community.

Discuss the advantages and disadvantages of this new influence on your community. Do you support or oppose the factory? Explain your position.

Economic activity is generally well received by any community **yet** there can be severe drawbacks such as pollution and traffic congestion.

Y = Sentence 1 = S1: This general sentence introduces the essay and uses a more advanced structure 'yet'.

24

I strongly feel the advantages far outnumber the downsides, and a community would be better welcoming the company.

O = S2: Here I place my opinion and my main reason. Sometimes you may need a second sentence to describe P2.

This essay will discuss both of these **views**, and use examples to demonstrate and describe the argument.

T = *TS3: Here is a universal sentence you can place if you have problems writing the stated amount of words:* **This essay will discuss both sides, using examples to demonstrate points and support arguments.**

Successful sports professionals can earn a great deal more money than people in other important professions. Some people think this is fully justified while others think it is unfair.

Discuss both these views and give your own opinion.

INTRODUCTION

Doctors, lawyers, accountants and other traditional activities are paid considerably well **yet** sport super stars are undoubtedly paid higher.

YS1: This general sentence introduces the essay and uses a more advanced structure 'yet'.

In modern society this causes an excess of controversy, however, I firmly believe that in a modern market economy each individual is entitled to a salary they deserve.

*OS2: Here I place my opinion and my **main** reason. Sometimes you may need a second sentence to describe P2.*

This essay will discuss both sides, using examples to demonstrate points and support arguments.

TS3: Here is a universal sentence you can place if you have problems writing the stated amount of words.

MORE EXAMPLES (TWO PART QUESTION)

Do you believe that experimentation on humans for scientific purposes is justified? Are there any alternatives to human

experimentation?

Testing products, chemicals, and procedures on humans is an important and controversial scientific matter yet alternatives do exist. These alternatives range from...

Should wealthy nations be required to share their wealth among poorer nations by providing such things as food and education? Or is it the responsibility of the governments of poorer nations to look after their citizens themselves?

Richer countries may provide money for vital services yet it is sometimes seen as the responsibility of the poorer countries themselves.

As most people spend a major part of their adult life at work, job satisfaction is an important element of individual well-being. What factors contribute to job satisfaction? How realistic is the expectation of job satisfaction for all workers?

Job satisfaction is determined by many factors yet some of these are undoubtedly out of reach for the majority of workers.

In some countries young people have little leisure time and are under a lot of pressure to work hard in their studies. What do you think are the causes of this? What solutions can you suggest?

Students are loosing leisure time due to various factors such as overworking, difficulty, and even poor planning, yet there are many solutions available.

ON THE ONE HAND........

Here we can substitute our 'firstly' and 'secondly' from the acronym and use 'On the one hand...'.

At the beginning of each paragraph.

You can write an essay now, using these two new points,

and the 13 sentences.

Or you can listen to the next chapter where we get more advanced.

ACTION

Some people prefer to spend their lives doing the same things and avoiding change. Others, however, think that change is always a good thing.

Discuss both these views and give your own opinion.

PLAN: As before, identify P1 and P2, build / plan the essay, using the 13 sentence plan.

Modify, the introductory sentence:

S1 = P1.......YET.......P2

Also, remember to change Firstly, Secondly to On the one hand....On the other hand....

MODIFYING SENTENCE 3

> This essay will discuss different views, using examples to demonstrate ideas and support arguments. **(If you can adapt this last sentence it will help you even more...)**
>
> **This essay will discuss different views, using examples related to P1 to demonstrate ideas, and P2 to support arguments.**
>
> This essay will discuss different views, using examples between market participants to demonstrate ideas, and comparisons with other subjects to support arguments.

6 Lists, Parallelism,

We're going to look at even more ways to improve on the 13sentence structure essay and learn sophisticated writing devices.

LISTS – 1 TOPIC SPECIFIC VOCABULARY

For the first sentence, it's the ideal opportunity to use a list to show the examiner your vocabulary. For example, if we get a question about pollution or climate change.

We can say something like, "Pollution, contamination and acid rain comprise of some of the largest environment challenges to any government and its citizens in the 21st century."

We take three words related to the topic and list them in succession.

For example, if we've got an essay about **crime**, we could say, "Delinquency, inequality and social discord comprise of some of the largest societal challenges to any government and its citizens in the 21st century."

If we have an essay about **globalization** or about economics or economic factors, we can say something like, "Production, competition and global trade comprise of some of the largest economic challenges to any government and its citizens in the 21st century."

If we've got an essay to write about **education or students**, we could say, "Students, high education and its cost are some of the largest challenges to any government and its citizens in the 21st century."

However, it must be **relevant.** If the essay asks us something about the past in one country and the past in another country, for example, it's impossible to discuss challenges to a government in the 21st century.

It's a good opportunity to show the examiner that we can write with a little bit of style and we can show the examiner some good vocabulary.

Using a list is a good introductory sentence but it has to be relevant.

LISTS 2 - EVEN

When we are making this list, we can improve it even further by pushing even before the last word in the list.
So, you can say, "Germany, France, and **even** Spain, have taken measures to avoid flooding in the future, blah, blah, blah." I said even Spain there because typically it's a dry country.

We would use EVEN, when the final component is unexpected.

South Africa, Brazil and even Scotland are experiencing warmer weather due to the heatwave....

PARALLEL STRUCTURES

Parallelism is a more sophisticated technique, but it's not difficult. Most of the examples I gave you before, were all parallel, and they flowed. Parallelism means that the sentence is balanced, if you used infinitive in your list you continue to do so. If you join an adjective phrase with a noun, it isn't parallel.

Compare:

"To vote, long demonstrations, and even going on strike, are some of the actions the public can take to make their voice heard."

Now, when it's parallel, and make sure that everything in my list matches as much as possible. If I use an infinitive in the first or for the first two, I will use an infinitive for the next one.

"To vote, to demonstrate, and even to strike, are some of the actions an electorate or the public can take to make their voice heard."

Compare:

"Families having less children, ageing populations, and people without jobs, are amongst the largest challenges a government and its citizens may face in the twentyfirst century."

Vs.

*"Declin**ing** birth rates, **ageing** populations, and ris**ing** unemployment, are amongst the largest socio-economic challenges to any government.*

I've used better vocabulary but I've also structured the whole sentence so it's parallel.

Pollution, contamination, and acid rain comprise of some of the largest (environmental) challenges to any government and its citizens in the twenty first century.

Polluting factories, contamination, and when it rains acid rain comprise of some of the largest (environmental) challenges to any government and its citizens in the twenty first century.

If we've got a list, it's an opportunity to show the vocabulary and make it a parallel list. Then it's going to flow.

The examiner's going to enjoy what he's reading or what she's reading.

That's another point as well that if you have problems, if you have difficulty whether to write his or her or he or she, the problem is in English in theory you're supposed to write he/she but that's clumsy. It's not that enjoyable to read.

For more information on Advanced writing structures, download the ADVANCED IELTS WRITING GUIDE

7 More Advanced Sentence Structures

Adding more sentences

Negative Constructions

Passive

Even if

HOW TO ADD MORE SENTENCES COHERENTLY

We have the basic structure, hopefully we have included a parallel list, the next step is make the essay longer.

We have the introductory sentence (p1), followed by the WHY?

Here we add another benefit: Furthermore.....or In addition,

This adds another argument and shows the examiner we can competently use 'linking devices'.

NEGATIVE CONSTRUCTIONS

Sentences with a negative construction look like this:

The government does not have adequate funding.

If we can say the same thing with less words, we're being more **succinct.**

The government lacks adequate investments.

The writing flows easier rather than having to use the negative constructions.

We can also use the negative verb:

The government does not have sufficient money.

We could say:

The government **lacks** sufficient money.

Or:

The government has **insufficient** money.

This is basically putting the verb into its negative form.

Here are some other prefixes that could be useful.

similar	dissimilar
smoker	non-smoker
conformist	nonconformist
able	unable
believable	unbelievable

The best way to do this is by testing, checking in the dictionary, looking for those, getting used to it, getting comfortable with them and starting to use them in your writing.

For more information on Advanced writing structures, download the ADVANCED IELTS WRITING GUIDE

PASSIVE

We touched on this before but I'll give you just a few more sentences just to give you some guidance. These are: It is widely believed. It can clearly be seen. It is without doubt that...

Also in the conclusion, we could use words like: to summarize, it can clearly be seen;

In summary; observing previous facts; therefore, considering the above arguments and explanations, I firmly believe...

EVEN IF

If you want to communicate a strong point, you could use the structure **'even if'** then use the condition. For examples:

Even if Australians prefer cricket to work, they are amongst the best workers in the world.

Even if unemployment means social challenges, there is opportunity to retrain and learn more skills.

Even if Americans never shower, they are still amongst the hardest workers around.

Even if English people prefer tea to coffee, Starbucks is still prospering.

You would probably use this in the middle of the paragraph and it would be, the second sentence of the paragraph.

8 Hedging, Repetition, Examples.

Have a look at this sample essay. Can you see the problems?

> For example, the information gained from people in other countries with people from various cultural backgrounds, always improves their efficiency at their workplace when practically applied. Consequently, people are able to attain their goals with less difficulty.

There are three problems with this text.

1. Hedging: The text makes a sweeping assumption.

> For example, the information gained from people in other countries with people from various cultural backgrounds, **always** improves their efficiency at their workplace when practically applied. Consequently, people are able to attain their goal with less difficulty.

Always = 100% certain, it is impossible to be so certain, especially in essay writing.

To 'hedge' we could say:

...the information gained from people in other countries with people from various cultural backgrounds, **usually** improves their efficiency...

...the information gained from people in other countries with people from various cultural backgrounds, **more often than not** improves their efficiency...

2. Repetition: The same words are used numerous times.

> For example, the information gained from **people** in other countries with **people** from various cultural backgrounds, always improves **their** efficiency at **their** workplace when practically applied. Consequently, **people** are able to attain **their** goal with less difficulty.

The remedy is to substitute these words for synonyms and reorganizing the sentence.

> For example, the information gained from **foreign nationals** in other countries with people from various cultural backgrounds, **usually** improves efficiency at **the** workplace when practically applied. Consequently, **when returning it is easier for them** to attain **their** goals.

3. **Examples:** The example is soft, vague and weak.

> For example, the information gained from people in other countries with people from various cultural backgrounds, always improves their efficiency at their workplace when practically applied. Consequently, people are able to attain their goals with less difficulty.

Why is it soft?

It lacks details such as: specific countries, numbers, dates, facts.

It fails to talk about any group, it says 'people'.

> For example, the information gained **by 'Korean' foreign nationals studying in the United States**, influences **their** efficiency at work, largely thanks to the interaction with other cultures and practices. Consequently, when returning they are usually able to attain their goals with less difficulty.

EXAMPE 2

Have a look at this sample paragraph. Can you see the problems?

> On the one hand it is undeniable that an individual has to make sacrifices when deciding to go to a foreign land to study. Families and friends have to be left behind. New customs and lifestyles have to be adopted and failure with this, results in frustration and even depression. Moreover, the difficulty to find a job for tuition fees puts intense pressure on students. As a result, at times, people return back to their home town without gaining any certificate and knowledge and end up taking drugs and have depression.

On the one hand it is undeniable that an individual has to make sacrifices when deciding to go to a foreign land to study. Families and friends have to be left behind. New customs and lifestyles have to be adopted and failure with this, <u>results in frustration and even depression *1.</u> Moreover, the difficulty to find a job for tuition fees puts intense pressure on students. As a result, at times, people return back to their home town without gaining any certificate and knowledge and end up taking drugs and with depression. *2

*1.

results in frustration and even depression. Is this a fact? An opinion? Do you have numbers? Details to prove your point? Or can you hedge the sentence:

Solution:
Families and friends have to be left behind. New customs and lifestyles have to be adopted and failure with this, HAS BEEN KNOWN TO <u>result in frustration and even depression.</u>

*2
As a result, at times, people return back to their home town without gaining any certificate and knowledge and end up taking drugs and with depression.

The above sentence needs hedging:

As a result, at times, people OFTEN return back to their home town without gaining any certificate and knowledge and COULD end up taking drugs and with depression.

However, we have to ask is that REALLY LIKELY? Probably not. If we had said this sentence it makes it more believable.

As a result, studies show 35% of students returning from foreign education suffer from depression due to the pressure and expectation of finding employment.

BONUS: ADVANCED IELTS WRITING SKILLS

#1 – USE NEGATIVE FORMS

1. Countless studies were not able to indicate the benefits of such procedures.
(fail to)

The government lacks suitable infrastructure

2. It is argued it is not logical to learn English just solely from a book.

It is argued it is **illogical** to learn English **just** solely from a book.
It is argued it is **illogical** to learn English just from a book.

3. After a very long time various factors are not available.

After a **very** long time various factors are **unavailable.**
After a long time various factors are **unavailable.**

4. Those students who can not organise their study time efficiently in the time
allocated will always suffer really bad consequences. (in 9 words clue: punish)

Those students unable to organise their study time efficiently in the time allocated will always suffer really bad consequences.
Students **unable** to organise their time efficiently will be **punished.**

5. Nobody was able to conduct an analysis of the blood in the office because the office had not enough pieces of equipment. (two modifications).

Nobody **could** conduct an analysis of the blood in the office because in the office there was **insufficient** pieces of equipment.

Nobody **could** conduct an analysis of the blood in the office because there was **insufficient** equipment.

6. We were not unable to decide to do the necessary research needed. -
(Reduce to 7 words).

We could decide to do the necessary research **needed**.
We could decide to do the necessary research.

7. Society at large has not got any direction. (Reduce to 6 words use: lack).

Society at large **lacks a** direction.

8. On the other hand it is not possible to argue the following points.

On the other hand it is **impossible** to argue the following points.

9. The government has not got infrastructure that is not suitable. (5 words)

The government has **unsuitable** infrastructure.

10. The local government did not invest in the community for six years.

The local government **failed to** invest in the community for six years

21 BAND 9 ESSAYS

ESSAY 1

Some people think that secondary school children should study international news as one of the school subjects. Other people think that it is a waste of valuable school time.

Give reasons for your answer and include any relevant examples from your own knowledge or experience.

P1 complete waste of time, dangerous difficult for news to be neutral. --EG Fox news – conservative, right wing, could impact child's beliefs and actions.

P2 waste of time, news is usually negative, if it bleeds it leads, studies show 85% of headlines are related to murder, war, natural disasters, terrorism.

The importance of global media appears to increase year after year, so much so there have been calls to introduce news channels into the classroom. I believe this to be politically dangerous and potentially damaging due to the nature of international media.

Firstly, considering the importance education has in a modern society, it is extremely worrying and dangerous to even consider substituting school subjects with international news. This is because the danger lies in choosing a correct balanced, unbiased and neutral news source, if one even exists. For example if a child spent their school days watching FOX NEWS, they would potentially have a skewed opinion of the world due to its unabashed right wing credentials. Therefore, changing a child's information diet from traditional subjects such as music, PE, or geography to watching a potentially partisan news channel is an extremely worrying and risky idea.

Secondly, if international news were to become a new subject it could have a detrimental emotional impact on young minds. This is because in general the majority of news is of a negative nature, hence the expression 'if it bleeds it leads'. For example, studies by the EFE News Agency show that 85% of headlines are negative in nature, usually referring to natural disasters, war, famine, etc. The logic of having these types of stories beamed into a school, to those of an impressionable age has to be challenged. Thus the obligation of watching news of a negative nature makes for a convincing argument against such an innovation.

To conclude, due to the risk from political influences, and the harsh reality of global news, I am strongly in favor of maintaining the current curriculum.

279

ESSAY 2

In some countries, using the internet in schools is getting more popular. Is this a positive or negative development?

As national barriers are slowly being broken down through trade, integration, and technology various organisations in society are being influenced especially by the internet. Nowadays practically all academic institutions are connected. Whether this is a beneficial or detrimental development is discussed in further detail below.

On the one hand there is ample evidence to suggest the benefits of the internet are increasing, especially related to an academic environment. This is because when a school is connected they have faster access to more information, furthermore it can bestow increases in efficiency. For example, in certain schools across the UK matters such as absenteeism, disciplinary procedures and general communication can be performed over the Internet through email. Therefore it is clear that being connected to the world wide web entails positive implications.

On the other hand, being connected to the internet has grave dangers and could even lead to an over reliance. This is due to the fact that undesirable facets of society have potential access to innocent children. Furthermore getting the into habit of consulting 'Google' for answers may be argued as putting too much faith into the hands of technology companies. For example, due to modern marketing technique such as SEO and SEM it is not difficult to tamper with search engine rankings. Therefore the over reliance on technology instead of traditional knowledge could be questioned.

To conclude, there are both negative and positive aspects to consider, however due to the wealth of information, the

41

conveniences that have been gained so far, I am strongly of the opinion that school internet connectivity is a positive development.

ESSAY 3

Some people say that restaurants are a waste of time. They claim that preparing food at home is cheaper, more economical and healthier.

Home preparation of meals was the traditional way of consuming most meals of the day. However large scale changes in the workplace have been reflected in the changing eating habits of society. Some would argue these are negative developments however I strongly disagree and have stated below with examples why this is not the case.

Firstly restaurants are most definitely not a waste of time, in fact they are widely consider to save time, hence the category 'fast food'. Their popularity in serving food on demand in a quick manner can not be refuted, largely due to their by their meteoric rise and conquer of international food markets. All though sophisticated marketing campaign have been employed, building global powerhouses such as MacDonalds cannot just be explained by marketing prowess. The convenience factor at eating at such restaurants infers one actually saves time rather than wasting it.

Secondly, preparing food at home is said to be healthier however, that would largely depend on what is being prepared. Furthermore, due to changing socio-graphic factors, such as longer working weeks, and more women entering the work place, traditional skills such as home cooking are disappearing. The cost of eating out has fallen considerably over the last ten years also. In the UK for example, in most cities which have large student districts not only is it more convenient to eat in restaurants it is actually cheaper than home cooking. Therefore, due to recent changes in society what was traditionally expensive has become inexpensive and invaluable for large parts of the society.

It can be clearly seen from the arguments above that eating out has become part of modern society and has numerous benefits over the traditional approach. To conclude I am of the opinion that this is a positive development.

ESSAY 4

Communication is less between family members of late. Do you agree or disagree?

As modern life is constantly changing it is said that family communication is breaking down. I agree that communication between family members has decreased mainly for two reasons. Firstly the role of technology and the internet has increased dramatically. Secondly, there has been a large shift in socio-demographics over the last fifty years.

Modern communication technologies and inventions such as the internet, mobile phones and personal computing have fundamentally altered the family. It is now common for adolescents to spend more time engaged in social media and the internet than actually communicating with their family members. The average teen in the west now spends over forty hours a week on the internet, it is doubtful they spend the same amount talking with their family.

Demographic changes over the last half century such as more house wives entering the workplace is another example of reduced family ties. In my city it was common place for the mother to pursue a career and pay for a child minder. This modern and increasing trend, especially in the western world has almost become the norm. Compared to a traditional model of sixty years ago this relatively new concept is another example of the reduced time spent for communication within a family.

To conclude both technological and demographic factors have and will continue to erode family communication. These two facets are the main culprits for the reduction of time spent conversing between family members, and the trend will most likely continue as more societies move towards a western economic model.

ESSAY 5

Advertisement is harmful for society, and for that reason people need to ban advertising. Do you agree or disagree with this statement? Explain your position.

Whether advertising innocently informs or misleads the masses has been debatable since its inception around the industrial revolution. Although advertising has become more sophisticated calling for an outright ban is close to censorship and borders on the ridiculous. Firstly there are laws that prevent misleading consumers, secondly as suppliers and buyers are now separated it is actually needed.

In developed countries powerful consumer watch bodies or self governing agencies are set up to avoid any harm to the consumer. In the UK there is an industry self regulating body called the Advertising Standards Agency which deals seriously with any complaints from the public. This agency is extremely strict with members so as to avoid unwanted heavy handed government intervention. Due to this self regulatory model it is questionable whether adverts could be close to being harmful to society.

Secondly, since the industrial revolution consumers are increasingly separated from producers, thus creating an information gap. Take the New Zealand Kiwi, their branding and advertising ensures a seal of quality which is trusted on the other side of the world in the UK. Without this communication from farmers in New Zealand the consumer could be duped into buying lesser quality produce. Banning this interaction between buyer and seller would be a disservice for consumers.

It can be clearly seen that it would be difficult for advertising to be harmful to the consumer due to self regulation, and that a ban would inflict more harm than good. However the positive impact of advertising on a society largely depends on its regulation, so sensible self governing is a prerequisite.

ESSAY 6

Some ex-prisoners commit crimes after being released from the prison. What do you think is the cause? How can it be solved?

Criminal punishment has become more civil compared to traditional methods however its effectiveness for behaviour reform is regularly questioned. The fact that various criminals are repeat offenders and find themselves in and out of jail is testament to a flawed punishment. The first paragraph will focus on why prison harms society, the second paragraph will propose a solution as to how the problem can be solved.

Jailing is a logical solution that should keep them out of society unfortunately it actually promotes a criminal career. Concentrating society's worse in one place is similar to holding a crime seminar for daily networking. Drug barons and gang leaders are notorious for recruiting while serving prison sentences. Therefore a criminal may enter as a car thief and leave as a fully fledged loyal soldier in a crime syndicate.

One possible solution would be to send first time offenders to do community service in the region they inflicted damage. In my local town petty crime is punished with terms such as litter picking, street cleaning and rubbish collection. Performing these tasks instils a sense of pride and eliminates the time spent with other criminals. Less networking and high level interactions would clearly reduce illegal opportunities for the offender therefore making them less likely to commit another crime.

In conclusion current correctional facilities promote criminal activities and are the root of the problem. The solution is limiting the chances and scale of criminal interaction with a different style of punishment. A drastic reform is necessary to enable society to deal with these challenges and to help criminals rehabilitate.

ESSAY 7

In many countries recently young single people have been living far from their parents, from the time they began studies or work and until they married. Do you think there are more advantages or disadvantages to this trend?

Student and worker mobility are ever increasing trends, their drivers being either local circumstances or the desire and curiosity to explore. In the current economic climate it has become more common to relocate. Although there are costs and cultural challenges I believe the advantages far outweigh the disadvantages.

Firstly there is the cost of having to move and possibly live in the new city without having secured work first. However with careful planning such as organising work before arrival through the internet, and sound financial preparation these factors can be mitigated. For example the Erasmus grant is a European funding facility to assist students who are interested in experiencing a semester in a foreign country. Once overcoming the financial hurdles the migrant student or worker has opened the doors to a richer educational experience or an improved economic future than awaited at home.

Secondly there will undoubtedly be cultural challenges nevertheless these must be seen as an advantage to relocating. For example overcoming a language barrier maybe painful at first however the long-term benefits of having learnt the language are incredible. This is another clear advantage of relocating away from ones home town.

To conclude, with careful planning to reduce initial expenses the financial disadvantage can be drastically reduced. In addition a second language and a cultural education are clearly greater than the cost of early challenges in a country. Due to these beneficial factors out numbering the drawbacks this trend can only continue to grow.

ESSAY 8

Paying more money is the only possible motivation to make employees work harder and to increase their productivity. Do you agree? Give reasons and include relevant examples.

Motivation in the workplace has being a topic of debate since the inception of the employer – employee relationship, the discussion frequently centres on the financial aspects. Although it is a logical assumption that higher wages should infer higher output it is not always the case. My viewpoint is that there are other factors at play for example psychological motivators such as part ownership and company leadership.

Firstly, part ownership is based on the concept that if you have a personal investment in the future of the company you are likely to want to ensure the success of the entity. Facebook for example is thirty percent owned by its employees through stock options. Owning a portion of the company where you work instils a sense of ownership which motivates one to think of the company as their own. If you have control over the destiny of the company it will undoubtedly motivate you to think twice when performing your daily tasks.

Secondly, leadership is often cited as a critical factor for motivating employees and can have a profound effect on the workplace. Consider Steve Jobs, he cultivated a legion of followers and employees by demanding that his company made products the employees would be proud of. Here the staff are motivated by non monetary values so increasing their salaries would have a negligible effect.

Leadership and part ownership are clear examples of increasing productivity via other means than simply increasing wages. To conclude, I strongly disagree that higher wages would result in staff working harder.

ESSAY 9

Some people are of the opinion that children should be rewarded for good behaviour. Others think they should be punished for bad behaviour. Discuss both views and give your personal opinion and reasons.

The debate over a child's moral education is difficult due to the various view points each party holds. The question of discipline is exceptionally important, moreover whether to treat good behaviour with a neutral attitude or to just focus on correcting incorrect actions. My personal opinion is that any positive actions ought to be immediately recognised by the parent and vice versa for negative conduct. This balanced approach makes for a more positive outcome for both the child and family.

Firstly rewarding a good act immediately signals a positive reaction in the child's brain which should encourage the child to want to behave similar in the future. Failure to recognise such behaviour leaves the child with the same emotional feeling as if they had done nothing. Therefore rewarding the child regularly for good behaviour enforces the action making it more likely to repeat itself in the future.

Secondly punishing the son or daughter is also necessary, failure to discipline could have serious consequences in the future. For example if a child has no clear concept of respect for elders or authority it is quite possible to encounter more serious problems later in life. This pattern is prevalent in marginal neighbourhoods throughout the world. Therefore it is essential to immediately discipline the child whenever witnessing an unruly act so as to enforce the correct behaviour from an early age.

To conclude both bad and good actions need to be recognised and dealt with immediately to correct or encourage the future actions. Failure to do either of these could result in a less fortunate life or a youth who rarely performs any good acts for anyone. Therefore it is critical that both types of behaviour are recognised dealt with accordingly for the benefit of the child in the future.

ESSAY 10

Many governments in the world spend large amounts of money on art which helps to develop quality in people's life. However, governments should spend money on other things rather than art. Do you agree or disagree? Give your opinion.

Societies with a heritage in the 'arts' have long been considered culturally sophisticated and advanced. However with the recent financial crisis this lavishness and expense should be questioned. Tax payers money has to be spent practically rather than on cultural endeavours. Firstly not everyone in society appreciates art and secondly employment should take precedence.

Art can bring quality into ones life if you are interested. Amongst a society art-lovers are typically in the minority and other activities such as sport are more popular. Take football for example, across the globe it is obvious that there are more people watching matches in stadiums than looking at sculptures or art. This fact makes it impossible that art can bring quality into a community if the galleries hold little interest for the region.

Secondly the resources diverted to such projects comes from the public and should be spent in a way that benefits them. Commissioning or purchasing art is an insult to tax payers who endure poor high unemployment such as those in Newcastle, UK. This city suffers from historically high unemployment yet the council commissioned a large sculpture called 'The Angel of the North'. Financing a job creation project would undoubtedly have been more practical for the local community.

To conclude I believe that it is an unjust affirmation that art brings quality into ones life and agree that the money should be spent elsewhere. This is because art expenditures only benefit a small minority and secondly the expense involved should benefit the majority. Ideally in the future governments will recognise that quality in a person's life derives from a decent opportunity in life, not a sculpture.

ESSAY 11

Some people believe that children's leisure activities must be educational, otherwise they are a complete waste of time. Do you agree or disagree? Give reasons for your answer and include any relevant examples from your experience.

To derive a double benefit from anything is considered a bonus and this is especially the case when discussing leisure activities for children. The idea to fusion both education and entertainment into one activity is a goal of many educators, some would even believe that failure to do this makes the activity pointless. Drawing from examples in Sweden and reviewing games such as Pokemon I firmly believe that all activities should have an educational value.

Leisure activities are a perfect time to take advantage of the receptiveness in a child's mind, some countries are adamant about this. Take Sweden for example, for various years they have legally stipulated that all children's toys sold in the country should have some educational value. In addition, for such a rule to be passed it must be upheld by scientific research. Therefore the advantage of incorporating an education element into toys is scientifically proven.

On the other hand, across the UK children were wasting their time collecting and learning all the statistics of each creature on each Pokemon card. If however these cards had been inter wined with more educational data the child could have simultaneously gained a more practical education. Due to the child learning large swathes of irrelevant and useless information it can be argued that the time would have been better spent with real facts and figures on the cards.

To conclude, scientific evidence from Sweden and fantasy

games such as Pokemon with little educational value are two clear reasons why children's leisure activities should have an element of learning involved.

ESSAY 12

Some people think high school graduates should travel or work for a period of time instead of going directly to study at university. Discuss the advantages and disadvantages of both approaches. Give reasons for your answer and include any relevant examples from your own knowledge or experience. You should write at least 250 words.

It is common for a student to take a gap-year in a foreign country or even work for a year prior to university. Whether a student should engage in travelling or working before embarking on a formal qualification has been a topic of debate for various years. Firstly the advantages of such activities will be discussed, followed by all the economical disadvantages one encounters on such endeavours.

The benefits of resisting university for a year to travel or work open the students mind to new worlds, such as having responsibility at work or learning a new language abroad. Having spent a year in Australia prior to university I learnt how to look for work, become responsible with finances and other essential life skills such as cooking. Upon starting university various tasks such as money management and employment were second nature thus allowing more time for studies. Without having gone abroad university life would undoubtedly be more challenging.

The disadvantages are mainly cost related, the airfare, travel insurance, national insurance and personal living costs are large sums. However finding another opportunity to go abroad is difficult once the pattern of normal life is resumed. In addition it also an opportunity to experiment with different jobs before choosing a career at university. Therefore there is a considerable advantage of taking a year out before higher education.

To conclude, the main disadvantages are the costs involved, however the benefits dramatically outweigh the disadvantages. Time should be spent wisely as it can never be recuperated unlike money which can be spent and earned.

ESSAY 13

Should education and healthcare be free of charge and funded by the government, or should it be the responsibility of the people to pay for these services? Discuss the above and give your opinion using examples.

A healthy and educated society is the backbone of any successful society, however, deciding who is to provide this is a sensitive topic. I strongly believe the government should be held responsible to provide these services for two reasons. Firstly the entire society benefits and secondly the whole population is currently paying for the services. However, if one prefers extra services they should be prepared to pay for it themselves.

Firstly, education is **largely considered** a basic right, a population unable to calculate, read, write or even learn would be doomed in such a competitive global economy. Globalisation has increased competition and shifted the emphasis to knowledge, information and science. A state education should therefore be freely available to everybody. However people wish to purchase private education, this should also be allowed or even encouraged. Private education reduces the strain on public services and provides a source of tax revenue for the government, in effect subsidising state education.

Secondly, health services must undoubtedly be available to all because the entire nation are paying taxes and therefore should not be excluded from any service. Take the NHS in the UK for example, this organisation caters for the entire population and no private medical insurance is needed. Unfortunately waiting lists can be long and service is occasionally slow, therefore some purchase private medical insurance for a faster service. This reduces the workload of the public sector.

To conclude, I believe both healthcare and education are basic fundamental rights, necessary for any advanced society and therefore the responsibility should lay with the government. Nevertheless if individuals require more than the standard level they should be prepared to pay for it.

277

ESSAY 14

Crime is a big problem in the world; many believe that nothing can be done to prevent it. To what extent do you agree or disagree? Give your own opinion.

Crime **is unquestionably one of the most prevailing and** worrying **aspects in any society and** its prevention **should be taken seriously**. Crime prevention can be executed in various ways, firstly through a sustained honest presence in the community and secondly through international cooperation.

A local presence by incorruptible law enforcement authorities **may be costly, however, the long term investment would pay dividends in the future**. A safer region would encourage trade, investment and set an invaluable example for younger generations. For example crime has dramatically been reduced in the Favelas around Rio de Janiero in Brazil. This was achieved largely **through the government committing large funds of money** to stationing police headquarters in and around the slums. **These financial expenditures greatly benefited the community.**

Secondly, due to the large scale severity and global impact crime has in some areas of the world, global cooperation is critical. **Operating in a different way would incur significant financial losses and render any expenditure futile.** For example Somalian pirates in Africa have reigned terror amongst many ocean transport companies in the area. Only through large scale international cooperation was policing the area possible. Therefore crime reduction can be attributed to a joint effort between countries.

To conclude illegal activities are a costly and dangerous fact in the present global economy, however, **through large scale government investment** prevention is an attainable goal.

Also spreading the expense through international cooperation
the **resources invested can be significantly more effective**
in reducing criminals effectiveness abroad.
248

ESSAY 15

Some people think that all children should learn geography in school. However, some others think that learning subjects more relevant to life is more important.

With constant modifications in school curriculum and constant changes in society the question of whether to maintain or drop geography is an interesting topic. I believe there would be severe consequences if geography were to disappear, mainly due to the understanding and open-mindedness that is derived from such studies.

Firstly, with **evermore** complex geopolitic strategies being played out, it can be considered extremely valuable to have the ability to identify the location of these events without checking on a map. Religious and border conflicts are amongst the most common sources of news events and a lack of knowledge as to where these events are being played out can be considered ignorant. For example, areas such as the middle east are constantly in the news. Therefore, by being merely aware of their location in the world, readers or viewers can greatly increase their understanding of the conflict.

Secondly, making geography compulsory in the schools would most likely encourage students to travel later in life. This is because geography can bring to light options you may not have known existed previously. For example, historically England has been the top destination to learn English, however in recent times students have learnt about more economical options such as Malta or Ireland. Therefore, without a sound geographical knowledge of Europe, these options could have been overlooked.

To conclude, removing geography from the school curricula would reduce a student's ability to fully assimilate global events in the media. Furthermore, removing the subject could indirectly reduce the amount of perceived options available to students.

ESSAY 16

Today, the quality of life in large cities is decreasing. Discuss the causes and solutions.

The global phenomenon of urbanisation from the beginning of industrialisation to the present day has brought opportunity and prosperity, albeit at a cost in the quality of life. With an increasing city population, the complexity of the challenges also increases, the causes and solutions for this are outlined below.

The causes for the decrease in the quality of life are paradoxically the prosperity endowed on such metropolitan centres. Their growth is largely due to the increase of opportunities on offer, which in turn increases their attractiveness, essentially they are trapped in a positive self enforcing cycle. However, this eventually leads to a decrease in the quality of life as the city can experience overcrowding, exorbitant property prices, and increased vulnerability to terrorist attacks. For example the density of London makes it a more efficient place to attack, when compared to a smaller city such as Bradford. Therefore, due to continuous growth and prosperity, urban citizens, especially the less well off, often experience a lower standard of living.

Considering the solutions, greater investment in public transport would ease traffic congestion, as would bike lanes. In theory this would reduce air pollution, and possibly improve the well-being of the population if they did adopt a more active lifestyle and cycle to work. To counter violent terrorist attacks, cities could embark on CCTV installations, so as to closely monitor for threats. For example, it is said, the CCTV in London has foiled many potential attacks, and therefore greatly increased the security of its citizens.

To conclude, a wealthy city attracts large population inflows, which then cause pressure on existing infrastructure and security. Various solutions exist to mitigate such drawbacks, nevertheless an indefinite solution has yet to be found.

ESSAY 17

Some people think that it is acceptable to use animals in medical research for the benefits of human beings, while other people argue that it is wrong.

Over centuries humans have experimented with many different chemicals, products, and processes, with the final aim of bettering our conditions. Testing products on animals most likely dates back centuries, however, in modern society it is a controversial point. Below is an outline of circumstances when it could be considered acceptable and unacceptable.

Firstly, it is clear that major advances in fighting disease, viruses and illnesses would not have been made without testing products on animals. This is because it is inhumane to test the products on healthy human beings, likewise using computer modelling to predict reactions is only a recent possibility and still not as reliable as testing on animals. Therefore without experiments on animals, breakthroughs in medicine would have been impossible, and most would agree the price paid has been worth it.

Conversely, it could be argued that medical research carried out for mere cosmetic ends is undoubtedly not worth the lives of innocent animals. This is largely for two reasons, firstly a large body of research is said to have been built up previously from past experiments, and secondly there are alternatives such as dermatological testing or using natural ingredients. For example, retail chains such as Lush and The Body Shop have both made fortunes by positioning themselves as natural solutions against animal testing. Therefore due to the end rationale for testing on animals, and the alternatives available, it is clear it is completely unjustifiable in this situation.

To conclude animal welfare can be side-stepped when the

situation is threatening humans and computer alternatives are simply too premature. Nevertheless, when the research has rather fickle motives and viable alternatives do exist, in these cases the loss of animal's lives in inexcusable.

ESSAY 18

Most of the schools are planning to replace sports and exercise classes with more academic sessions. What is your opinion on this change? How does this change will affect children's life in your view?

The debate between where to allocate valuable teaching resources probably started with the first educational institutions. In present day society the conflict continues and rightly so. In my opinion converting sports classes to more traditional subjects has two significant advantages. Firstly it is a more effective use of a students time, secondly in the future, academic skills are more useful.

Switching time spent on sport in a school to time spent on more academic activities is a wise and cost effective solution. Firstly, academic studies are inherently less expensive to perform when compared to physical education. For example, to play almost any sport one has to invest in the appropriate equipment, ranging from shorts, t-shirts to rackets and balls. Furthermore excess time is spent in the changing rooms or washing afterwards. In more traditional subjects, students merely enter the classroom and are learning within minutes.

Secondly sport can be argued as an activity practised naturally by children, especially boys. In every school at break time many children engage in energetic activities, whereas hardly any are studying algebra, biology or physics. Because these subjects are less popular more resources should be allocated to teaching them. In addition, academic skills could be argued as more important due to the small amount of people in society currently using sport skills in a work environment. Thus focussing on skills demanded by the labour market would benefit students lives dramatically in the future.

To conclude, young learners going through school would finish much better prepared for life avoiding sport tuition. Furthermore they would have taken full advantage of their school years through more time spent learning.

271

ESSAY 19

Improvements in health, education and trade are essential for the development of poorer nations. However, the governments of richer nations should take more responsibility for helping the poorer nations in such areas.
To what extent do you agree?

Undoubtedly governments of developed nations should share the responsibility of helping less fortunate nations. Different measures exist, ranging from market access to direct financial payments or even medical assistance. This essay will explain why certain measures are inherently better than other methods.

Firstly, the most adequate manner to assist the lesser developed countries is not through health or education 'hand-outs'. This method is flawed and only offers temporary relief from long term challenges, also this assistance can be cut at any moment, leaving the country stranded. For example economical help from the UK to disadvantaged regions in Africa has gradually been reduced since the onset of the financial crisis. Although some parts of the country maybe better educated or in better health the benefit was short lived thus leaving the country to look for other donors.

Commerce is without doubt the most essential type of assistance that can be given. If the lesser developed country has the opportunity to develop trade it will build strong capabilities to serve it for the long term. These strengths can develop the local economy and are more reliable than education or health. For example, while trading with the richer country the government can search for other foreign markets to trade with. This would offer more stability and diversification for the nation.

To conclude, assistance is definitely necessary for the poorer regions however 'hand-outs' are short term solutions. The optimum solution is to offer market access so the region can produce products and generate regular income.

251

ESSAY 20

Women can do everything that men can and they even do it better. They also can do many things that men cannot. But there is a fact that their work is not appreciated as men's although they have to sacrifice a lot for their family, and career... So someone said: " A woman's place is in the home. What do you think?

Women and men have had different roles in the community since the beginning. Under modern pretexts these differences are slowly converging. However due to the genetic inheritance and socio demographic components, these differences do exist.

Firstly, men are undoubtedly better adapted genetically to perform physical tasks. Therefore the assumption that women can match men in everything is clearly flawed. The difference between their physical abilities is clearly demonstrated in the sporting arena. Take for example the Olympics, or any international sporting event. It can be clearly seen that these competitions the genders are separated due to inherent differences between the sexes.

Secondly, it has been argued that women are less appreciated in society due to their traditional roles in the home. This statement is true to a certain extent because it largely depends on the society. In certain traditional societies in Africa, females working is frowned upon and is seen as neglecting the family. Whereas in Afghanistan, in general, females are allowed to do little else but stay at home, being a housewife. Consequently a woman's value is largely dictated by the society, culture and history. Nevertheless to state that her place is in the home is widely considered sexist in modern western societies.

To conclude differences do certainly exist, however these

are largely through nature. Also, the role women may have is usually dictated by other factors such as religion or society, not ability.

ESSAY 21

The world is consuming natural resources faster than they can be renewed. Therefore, it is important that products are made to last. Governments should discourage people from constantly buying more up to date or fashionable products. To what extent do you agree with this statement?

Over the last 30 years the West has witnessed the East strive for a larger 'piece of the economic pie', aiming for similar living standards to the EU and US. This has increased pressure on natural resources and prompted suggestions for governments to limit consumption. This idea is severely flawed because it reduces product safety and 'building products to last would harm the poor.

Firstly, the suggestion that governments should discourage consumers from purchasing 'up to date products' would eliminate the opportunity to improve their safety. This is because as technology improves, new discoveries can be used to increase their utility. Take for example the car industry, here technology such as ABS brakes, air-bags, seat belts have all been derived from a constant flow of improvements. Therefore if the authorities were permitted to limit purchases, car companies would be reluctant to invest in new features, and safety would never improve.

Secondly, it is true we are consuming more, through ever increasing populations, nevertheless, the argument that 'products should be made to last' is redundant. If products were built stronger they would be more expensive. This would harm the less wealthy consumer, furthermore with modern technology these products can often be recycled at a later date anyway. Glass, plastic, paper, batteries, and even mobile phones are now collected to be re-purposed, reused and recycled. Therefore durable products are unnecessary and would harm lower income demographics.

To conclude it is clear that if the public sector were allowed to discourage consumption it would harm product improvements and ultimately consumer safety. Meddling with product durability would most likely harm the poor. Therefore I am strongly opposed to both of these notions.
278

ESSAY 22

Advances in health and biology and other areas of society in the last 100 years have transformed the way we live as well as postponing the day we die. There is no better time to be alive than now. To what extent do you agree or disagree with this opinion?

Biology is one of the most important areas of science due to its direct relationship to survival and health. Observing the rapid advances made, it has been suggested that it is presently the optimum time to be alive. I strongly agree with this affirmation for two reasons, firstly lives have been improved, and secondly risks have been reduced.

First, comparing life with a century ago it is possible to list new benefits available such as hospitals, doctors, medicines, diagnoses, donors, and transplants, all of which were extremely rare previously. Advances in the sciences have improved lives across society considerably. For example example, consider an operation in France several years ago whereby a woman received a complete face transplant. This would be unthinkable in 1910, therefore, due to science her life has undoubtedly improved.

Secondly, health risks have fallen incredibly, so much so that it is possible to visit tropical countries which previously carried considerable dangers. This is because traditionally preventative measures such as vaccinations, immunisation and prescription tablets did not exist. In addition over the last thirty years their cost has fallen rendering exotic travel available to almost anyone with the funds. Therefore modern science has increased the opportunities and reduced the risks related to travel, there has been no parallel in history.

To conclude, I strongly agree that biology and improvements in science have increased people's well being and their opportunities to explore the world. This is undoubtedly the first time in history such situations have existed.
250

ESSAY 23

"Prevention is better than cure". Out of a country's health budget, a large proportion should be diverted from treatment to spending on health education and preventative measures. To what extent do you agree or disagree with this statement?

A government has various responsibilities to its citizens, perhaps the most important would be health care. There are different approaches to this, namely prevention versus cure. This essay will explain why treatment is superior, using the case of tobacco as a clear example.

Firstly, health education has its limits. Over the last twenty years various western governments have attempted to discourage smokers by placing surgeon's warnings and revolting pictures. Yet smokers are still wont to light up, therefore seriously questioning government endeavours of prevention rather than cure. Nevertheless, through the same period cancer treatment has improved considerably even producing beneficial spin off discoveries for asthma suffers. Therefore treatment is not only more effective, it has also bettered other sectors of society.

Secondly, even if prevention has solid evidence of being effective there is the common case of patients suffering by pure chance. For example it is known that people can suffer from lung cancer having never smoked anything whereas someone smoking twenty a day can escape such illness. Therefore, even having followed government guidance, there would still be a need for treatment. In addition, if funds had been diverted from research for cures to education there would be little to help 'chance victims'.

To conclude, all though smoking has addictive elements, drawing from observations over various year it is clear that prevention has failed considerably. Furthermore, treatment can help those afflicted by pure chance, and even benefit patients with related challenges.

242

BAND 9 IELTS TASK 1
Writing task 1 (a letter)

Write a letter to a manufacturer to ask them to arrange production of a new item for you. Please say
- What item do you need?-
 Why do you need it?
You should write at least 150 words.

Dear Sir / Madam,

I am contacting you to organise production of new bicycle tyres because in the near future we will have exhausted existing stock levels.

Further to our successful marketing campaign sales have increased considerably and we are delighted to inform you that another campaign will start in May. We are expecting a surge in demand and therefore feel it necessary to implement all precautions to avoid complications in the supply chain.

With reference to the order it is important you understand the new industrial specifications as stated in the contract. We will require three boxes of the off-road heavy duty model (SE13344633), this line is new so please confirm via email or phone when the factory has started producing these. In addition, could you possibly send us samples of the raw materials to be used due to local regulations and product standards.

Kind Regards,

B. Worthington

BAND 9 IELTS ESSAY TASK 1
Writing task 1 (a letter)
Write a letter to your manager and ask for his/her comments regarding the article which will be published in a famous magazine next month. In this letter, you should say
- What have you written the article about?
- Why did you write it?
- What makes it so special?
You should write at least 150 words.

Dear Ben,

I have recently written a small piece about out companies new product line, the article will hopefully be featured in Forbes this July. I have included all the relevant product details, specifications and applications of the product, including your idea and comments about the patent.

With Forbes having an international presence and access to the ideal target market of affluent North American males it will be perfect publicity. Exposure in such a high brow magazine is definitely a wonderful opportunity which can not be underestimated.

Due to the importance of this matter, and the fact you are directly quoted I would appreciate if you could offer your feedback prior to publishing in a months time. The information regarding the patent is of special importance since there is the company's intellectual property at stake.

If you have any questions please just ring my office directly and we can discuss the matter.

Thanks in advance,
Simon

BAND 9 IELTS ESSAY TASK 1
Writing task 1 (a letter)

A reporter complained about a new TV program that you like. Write a letter to the newspaper editor.
- Describe your point of view.
- Say what you like about the show and why.
- Ask the newspaper to take some action.
You should write at least 150 words.

Dear Mr Bradshaw,

I am contacting you regarding the article where you unfairly criticized Top Gear, namely Jeremy Clarkson. Understandably Mr Clarkson is not everyone's cup of tea, however publicly complaining then lambasting him and the show is unfair. Their difference of opinion is under no circumstances an excuse to write a letter of complaint.

Personally I feel that the shows ingenuity largely stems from the fact that their presenters are occasionally controversial and honest. This is unlike the modern TV shows which are bland, politically correct and just lacking any entertainment value for my liking.

I would be very grateful if you could in future editions of your newspaper 'The Echo' only publish positive articles about the programme. Failing this small request could you please refrain from any undue negative press.

Kind Regards,
B. Worthington

250 IELTS TASK 2 QUESTIONS

EDUCATION

Things like puzzles, board games and pictures can contribute to a child's development. What would you give a child to help him/her develop and why? Give details and examples in your explanation.

Do you think it is better for students to work before their university study? Why?
Use reasons and specific examples to support your choice.

Students perform better in school when they are rewarded rather than punished. To what extent do you agree or disagree? Discuss both views and give your own opinion.

Some people think that schools have to be more entertaining, while others think that their sole purpose is to educate. Which do you agree with?
Use specific reasons and examples to support your opinion.

Nowadays computer education is compulsory for your learners in most schools. Do you think this is necessary or will children acquire these skills naturally from their daily interaction with technology everywhere?
Provide your opinion and use specific reasons and examples to support your answer.

Some people believe that children should do organised activities in their free time while others believe that children should be free to do what they want to do in their free time. Which viewpoint do you agree with?
Use specific reasons and examples to support your answer.

Some people think that a person improves intellectual skills better

when doing group activities. To what extent do you agree?
Use specific details and examples to explain your view.

Compared to the past, more people are now studying abroad
because it is more convenient and cheaper than before. Do you
think this is beneficial to the foreign student's home country?
Use specific reasons and examples to support your opinion.

Some people think that children should be home schooled when
they are very young while others think it is better for them to attend
a kindergarten. Which do you think is better?
Use specific reasons and examples to support your answer.

Computers have become so advanced and interactive that
students in the future will have no need for a human educator in
the classroom. Do you agree? Why or why not?
Use reasons and specific examples to explain your answer.

In some countries, health care and education are only partially
funded by the government. Some people argue that the government
should be responsible for covering the full cost of these services.
Do you support or oppose the opinion? Explain your position.

Some students do very well at school and never have problems
while others fall behind. Are they capable of handling this challenge
themselves or should teachers and parents help them?
Use specific reasons and details to support your answer.

Doing an enjoyable activity with a child can develop better skills
and imagination than reading. To what extent do you agree?
Use reasons and specific examples to explain your answer.

University students nowadays have too much freedom and do not
study enough. To what extent do you agree and disagree? Explain
your opinion, using specific reasons and examples.

The internet has become so efficient and popular that many people
rely on it for learning. Some suggest that it could replace the use
of books as the main source of knowledge for education.

Do you support or oppose the opinion? Explain your position.

What do you think is the best way to find a job: by gaining more knowledge and education or through more practical skills?
Explain your choice, using specific reasons and details.

Do you think that education and training should be completely free or it is better to require fully paid tuition? Which way do you prefer?
Use specific reasons and examples to support your answer.

Students should be completely free to choose whether to study or play games. They should be allowed to manage their own time. Do you agree or disagree?
Use specific reasons and examples to support your position.

Some people think that real life skills like cooking, housekeeping and gardening should be included in the curriculum as compulsory subjects? Do you agree or disagree?
Explain your opinion, using specific reasons and details.

Childcare has always been of primary concern and importance. Do you think that courses designed to help mothers are necessary or can they acquire the essential knowledge through personal experience?
Use specific reasons and examples to support your opinion.

Gaming is argued to have a bad influence on young children but some people think that it could have a positive effect on them as well. Which view do you agree with?
Use reasons and specific examples to explain your answer.

Do you agree or disagree with the following statement? If students were given the choice between 'not to study' and 'study most of the time', they would choose 'not to study'.
Use specific reasons and examples to support your opinion.

School curriculum is selected by the central education authority rather than by the teachers, parents and students. Some believe that the latter should take part in the choice. Which viewpoint do

you agree with?
Use specific reasons and examples to support your answer.

In some countries, Physical Education is a compulsory subject for the leaving certificate. Some people suggest that this practice be abolished? Which view do you agree with? Explain your choice, using specific reasons and details.

Many universities have introduced tests for evaluation rather than the old written exams based upon lessons from books. What is your opinion?
Use specific reasons and examples to support your answer.

Some people say that school education is not useful and the essence of study can be acquired at home.
Do you agree? Why or why not?
Use reasons and specific examples to explain your answer.

Spending wisely and getting into the habit of saving from an early age is important. To what extent do you agree or disagree?
Use specific reasons and examples to support your position.

Modern trends in early education focus on an array of school projects and on developing natural skills through games and similar activities. Which do you consider the better approach and why?
Explain your choice, using specific reasons and details.

In recent years, online education is becoming more and more popular. What are the advantages and disadvantages of this phenomenon?
Use specific details and examples to explain your opinion.

Tuition for healthy children usually has top priority in most countries. However, teaching students with disabilities or mental issues is more difficult and even more important to support and develop. Which viewpoint do you agree with?
Use specific reasons and examples to support your answer.

GLOBALISATION

Some people believe that the most important aspect of their job is their salary. Others think that the job itself is the most important. What do you think is the most important aspect of a job? Include specific details and examples to support your choice.

Many people say that globalization and the growing number of multinational companies have a negative effect on the environment. To what extent do you agree or disagree? Use specific reasons and examples to support your position.

Why do you think social skills are now being emphasized by companies during the recruitment process? Give specific reasons and examples to support your answer.

In today's very competitive world, a worker has to possess multiple skills to succeed. Among the skills that a worker should possess, which skill do you think is more important, social skills or good qualifications?
Explain the reasons and provide specific examples to support your answer.

Do you think businesses should hire employees who will spend their entire lives working for the company?
Explain why do you agree or disagree. Use specific reasons and details to support your answer.

Would you prefer to stay in one company or change companies at one point in your career life? What are the advantages and disadvantages for both scenarios? Give specific details and examples to support your opinion.

Do you think that people who work online at home are more productive than office workers or the other way around? Give reasons and examples to support your answer.

Many countries now face an economic downturn so it is better for each country to focus on its own problems rather than helping other countries.

To what extent do you agree or disagree? Use specific reasons and examples to support your position.

Every country should produce enough of everything that the country needs so it should not rely on imports. Do you agree or disagree with this statement?

Use specific reasons and examples to support your position.

Some developed countries now have unemployment problems. Why do people still want to emigrate to these countries?

Give reasons and specific examples to explain your answer.

EQUALITY

Some people think women should be given equal chances to work and excel in their careers. Others believe that a women's role should be limited to taking care of the house and children. Which opinion do you agree with and why? Include specific details and examples to support your choice

Parents want to achieve balance between family and career but only a few manage to achieve it. What do you think is the reason? Discuss possible solutions and provide examples.

Nowadays both men and women spend much money on beauty care. This was not so in the past. What may be the root cause of this behaviour?
Discuss the reasons and possible results.

Some people give praise to famous scientists and mathematicians. Others think more highly of literary authors and artists than scientists or mathematicians. Which group of professionals do you regard more highly and why? Include specific details and examples to support your choice.

Men and women can never share the same responsibilities at home and in everyday life. Do you agree or disagree?
Use specific reasons and details to support your answer.

Some people think that not only should professional sports and cultural enterprises be sponsored by the government but also that amateur adult and children groups should get funding. Do you agree or disagree?
Use specific reasons and examples to support your position.

Professionals like doctors, teachers and lawyers contribute equally to society with non-professionals including entertainers and sports people. Thus, they should receive equal pay. Do you agree or disagree with this statement?
Use specific reasons and examples to support your position.

ENVIRONMENT

Environmental issues have always been an international problem because governments are not imposing harsh punishments against offenders. To what extent do you agree or disagree?
Support your answer with specific reasons and examples.

Managing global environmental issues should be handled by one organization on a global scale. To what extent do you agree or disagree?
Use specific reasons and examples to support your opinion.

Many agricultural lands are being converted into commercial centres. How does this affect the environment and the people's life style?
Discuss this situation and provide suggestions. Support your answer with specific reasons and examples.

Many efforts have been made by countries to address problems concerning the environment but, the situation has not improved. What are the possible reasons and results of this situation?
Discuss the situation and give suggestions.
Provide reasons and examples to support your answer.

Nowadays, it is possible to move ocean creatures from their natural habitat at sea and have them relocated in amusement parks for the purpose of people's recreation. Do you think the advantages of this development outweigh the disadvantages?
Explain your reasons and support them with specific examples.

The government should close companies that produce toxic waste materials without their own waste treatment facility in order to protect the environment. To what extent do you agree or disagree?
Use specific reasons and examples to support your position.

Many believe that companies behind oil and gas production promote new boundless opportunities while others fear the results from their intrusion in nature.

Discuss possible reasons, results and solutions.

Why do we need to prevent the extinction of some animals like dinosaurs and dodos if it is caused by natural processes? What is your opinion about this?

People produce more garbage than in the past. Explain how it is affecting us and the measures that could be taken to address the situation.
Provide specific examples and explanation to support your answer.

In modern times, some species of animals are slowly disappearing. Do you think that it is acceptable I for species to become extinct? What are the possible reasons and consequences of this extinction? Provide reasons and examples to explain your opinion.

Do you agree or disagree with the following statement? Protecting the Environment is the responsibility of the government.
Use specific reasons and examples to support your opinion.

Do you agree or disagree that the world was a better place decades ago that it is today? Why do you think so? Give specific details and examples to support your answer.

TECHNOLOGY

Do you think that technological advancement has brought more harm than good? Use specific reasons and details to support your answer.

What technologies did you use to help you in your studies? Describe how it has helped you. Use specific reasons and details to support your answer.

With the latest technological advancements, dating is now possible online. Would you recommend online dating for your single friends? What are the advantages and disadvantages of online dating? Site some examples to support your answer.

All inventions and discoveries like the discovery of fire and electricity have impacts on our lives so much so that people can no longer live without them. To what extent do you agree or disagree? Use specific reasons and examples to support your answer.

Traditional classrooms in the past held lectures with multiple participants. Now that technology makes it easier and faster for students to access information, the need for traditional classroom discussion is becoming less popular because the internet is a more effective method than the regular classroom.
Do you agree or disagree with this statement? What is your personal opinion?

Many big companies in the world are undergoing processes of modernization.

What are the benefits and consequences of this modernization? Explain the reasons and results of this change and provide specific examples.

Some people prefer to get the latest news through the internet or TV. Others still prefer to get the news from newspapers and magazines. Where do you prefer to read the news and why?

Include specific details and examples to support your choice.

What is technology for the environment; a destructive force or a solution? Do we need to stop using technology to save the environment? Why or why not?

Is life without technology less stressful? What is your opinion about living without technology?

Some people think that life has become easier with modern technology. Others argue that it is more difficult and dangerous. Discuss and give examples.

What do you think is the greatest contribution of your country in the field of science and technology? Describe it and explain why it is of great importance. Give details and examples in your explanation.

The -internet has a bigger impact on people's lives because it is more popular than television. Do you agree or disagree?
Use specific reasons and examples to support your position.

Is it good for children to start using computers from an early age and spend long hours on it? Discuss the advantages and disadvantages. Explain your choice, using specific reasons and details.

Experts claim that there is a way to tell if a child will become a criminal at an early age. If this was possible, what do you suggest should be done to prevent these children from becoming criminals? Explain your answer with specific reasons and examples.

Some products can be made quickly by a machine. Other items take a long time to be made by hand. As a buyer, which do you prefer and why? Give specific details and examples in your answer.

Some people think that face-to-face communication is better than other types of communication, such as letters, email or telephone calls. Which form of communication do you prefer and why? Give specific details and examples in your answer.

Internet and technology like mobile phones and laptops are connecting us to each other every hour of the day via networking sites and applications. Do you think it's an advantage or disadvantage? Explain your answer. Use specific reasons and details to support your answer.

Some companies spend a lot of money on scientific research and use animals for testing. Many argue that this is for a just cause while others say otherwise. Do the advantages of using animals in research outweigh its disadvantages?
Support your answer with specific reasons and examples.

E-mail is now the easiest way to communicate with families and friends all over the world. Some people say that it does not have the sincerity of hand written letters. Do you agree or disagree? Give specific details and examples to support your opinion.

With the speed and ease of viral communication do you think it will totally replace papers and letters in their old form? If that happens, will it be for the better?
Explain and provide specific reasons and examples to support your opinion.

There are opinions that technology and science are beneficial but also destructive. Due to technological advancement, mankind has irrevocably ruined nature and environment and affected the climate. To what extent do you agree or disagree?
Use specific reasons and examples to support your position.

In the future people will not need to have schools, galleries, museums or libraries because everything from education to culture and entertainment will be available online. Do you agree or disagree?
Use specific reasons and examples to support your answer.

Being literate in technology or the internet is so popular that many believe that it will no longer be necessary to read conventional books as the main source of material for education.
To what extent do you agree or disagree?

Use specific reasons and examples to support your position.

Advancement in technology helps to improve the standard of life. Meanwhile, according to data, while the average change in society in developing countries is positive, in richer countries this can be exactly the opposite. To what extent do you agree or disagree with this?

TRAVEL AND TRANSPORT

In many countries people tend to move overseas or move to a different part of their country after their retirement. Discuss why it is so and the outcomes of this situation.
Provide specific reasons and examples to support your opinion.

Some people prefer to use energy-saving modes of transportation like hybrid cars and bicycles. Others prefer the usual mode of transportation like buses and trains because it is fast and efficient. Which mode of transportation do you prefer and why? Use specific reasons and details to support your answer.

Low-price airlines lack most of the conveniences of normal air plane flights. However, the prices of the tickets are usually lower. Discuss negative and positive aspects of having lower rates of air plane tickets for travellers. Provide specific reasons and examples to support your response.

Is it good for families if parents need to travel a lot in their job or if they need to move to other cities? Is moving to a new location positive for children?
Discuss your opinion and support it with specific reasons and examples

Better driver education and information for better driving habits are better than heavier punishments for driving offences. To what extent do you agree or disagree?
Use specific reasons and examples to support your position.

Some people like to travel outside of their countries. Others would rather travel to the tourist spots in their own country first before travelling abroad. Which do you prefer to do and why? Include specific details and examples to support your choice.

In some cities although more and more people use public transport the roads are still crowded. How can this problem be solved?
Provide specific reasons and examples to support your opinion.

95

People are more mobile nowadays. They seldom live in one city all their lives. Why do you think this is happening? What are the consequences of this trend? Discuss the advantages and disadvantages of this situation. Provide specific reasons and examples to support your opinion.

In some countries the government promotes public transport as the primary means of transportation and discourages private vehicle ownership.
Discuss the advantages and disadvantages of this situation. Provide specific reasons and examples to support your opinion.

Compared to the past, people can now work in places that are far from their homes because of modern means of transportation. How has this affected the lives of workers?
Discuss the advantages and disadvantages of having modern transportation. Support your answer with specific reasons and examples.

Recent surveys show increased interest in relocation and travel to other countries. What may be the reasons for this trend and what will be the possible outcome from this behaviour?
Provide examples for your opinion.

HEALTH

In your own opinion, what do you think are the factors that contribute to longevity? List some examples and reasons to support your answer.

Some people think that keeping pets is good for children while others think it is dangerous and unhealthy. Which opinion do you agree with?
Discuss both options and give examples.

Even when poor countries get help from rich countries, hunger is still an issue.
Discuss probable causes and solutions.
Support your answer with specific reasons and examples.

Compared to the past, more younger adults take medications for degenerative diseases.
Provide specific reasons and examples to support your answer.

Today more countries import food from different parts of the world.
Discuss the advantages and disadvantages of this trend.
Provide specific reasons and examples to support your answer.

In some countries the population is ageing and the birth rate is declining. How will this affect society and how can it be prevented?
Give specific reasons and examples to support your answer.

Some people say that it is better to promote healthy lifestyles than spend so much money to treat obese people. To what extent do you agree or disagree?
Use specific reasons and examples to support your position.

More people now have children later in life. Some think it is not a good development for the family and for the country. Compare these two views.
Use specific reasons and examples to support your position.

Obesity is a serious problem in many countries, especially in rich countries. Discuss ways to solve the problem. Provide specific reasons and examples to support your answer.

More people are now trying out different varieties of food which results in consumption of ingredients from different parts of the world. Do you think this is a positive or negative development? Provide specific reasons and examples to support your opinion.

In some countries, health care and education are only partially funded by the government. Which do you think is better in terms of quality: free public healthcare and education or privately paid health care and education?
Provide specific reasons and examples to support your position.

Do you think that an ageing society will disappear? What are the advantages and disadvantages of having more old people in society?

Which is better: to have children earlier or later in a woman's life? What are possible reasons and effects of these two tendencies on a personal scale and for society in general?
Support your answer with specific reasons and examples.

Some people, including medical workers argue against using animals and humans for clinical tests while others think it is necessary. Which are you in favour of?
Provide specific reasons and examples to support your opinion.

Many people think that home cooked food is healthy, but many people still prefer eating out. Why is this so? Provide specific reasons and examples to support your opinion.

LAW AND ORDER

Nowadays there is an increase in social problems involving young people because more parents spent time at work than with their children.
To what extent do you agree or disagree? Give specific reasons and examples to support your answer.

In some countries, the number of shootings increase because many people have guns at home. To what extent do you agree or disagree?
Give specific reasons and examples to support your answer.

The number of refugees and immigrants is increasing. What are the possible causes and effects of this?
Provide specific reasons and examples to support your answer.

Nowadays you can find instructional videos for just about any crime you can think of. What possible effects can this have on individuals and society?
Provide specific reasons and examples to support your answer.

In many countries the age of criminals is getting lower. Give reasons and solutions to the problem.

Support your position with relevant examples.

In most countries military officers retire at the age of 45 while other people work as long as 65 to 70. Compare these two approaches.
Provide specific reasons and examples to support your position.

Some people believe that once a person becomes a criminal, he will always be a criminal. Do you agree with this statement?
Provide specific reasons and examples to support your opinion.

In some countries prisons are overcrowded which leads to many expenses for the government. To lessen the cost for prisoners' cost of living, reduced sentences are implemented. What do you

suggest could be done?
Provide specific reasons and examples to support your answer.

Some people are afraid to go out for fear of being robbed on the streets. Still, there are robberies that happen inside houses. What do you think is the best thing a person can do to ensure his/her own security? Use specific reasons and examples to support your answer.

In some countries prisoners are allowed comfortable accommodation, good food, and healthcare. Do you think this is appropriate? To what extent do you agree or disagree?
Give specific reasons and examples to support your position.

More people are now behaving more violently in society than before. Can this behaviour be prevented?
Discuss the causes and reasons for this trend.
Provide examples to support your opinion.

In some countries police officers do not carry guns. How does this affect the manner they implement law and order? Discuss the advantages and disadvantages of having a gun.
Provide specific reasons and examples to support your opinion.

Some people think that with combined effort on the part of the government and society crime can be completely eradicated, while others argue that this is completely hypothetical and that crime has always been present in societies even in ancient times. Compare these two views. Which do you agree with?
Use specific reasons and examples to support your answer.

Crime is a growing problem on a global scale. Some think that crime prevention rather than punishment is the key to solve the problem. To what extent do you agree or disagree?
Give specific reasons and examples to support your position.

Special programs for social integration and help are better alternatives than harsher prison sentences for minor crimes. Do you support or oppose this opinion?

Explain your position.

LANGUAGE AND CUTURE

Some people think it is better to spend and enjoy their money once they earn it. Others think it is better to save their money and enjoy it in the future. Which stand do you agree with and why? Use specific reasons and examples to support your opinion.

Some people think it is alight to spend money for their wants, such as a new car or the latest gadget. Others think it is better to save their money and only buy what they really need. Which opinion do you agree with and why? Give specific details and examples in your answer.

Some parents do not allow their children to watch TV during school days. Others allow their children to watch TV as long as their school work is finished. Which approach do you agree with and why? Include specific examples and details in your explanation.

Some parents prefer to have their children be raised by their grandparents. Some prefer to raise them on their own. Which would you prefer and why? Include specific details and examples to support your choice.

Some parents allow their teenage children to live independently, away from home. Other parents don't want their teenage children to live away from them. Which do you think is better and why?
Use specific reasons and details to support your answer.

Some people believe that watching television is bad for children. Other people believe that watching television is educational for children. Which opinion do you agree with and why?
Give specific details and examples in your answer.

Some people believe that people behave differently when they wear different clothes, while others do not believe that clothes influence the way people behave. Which opinion do you agree with and why? Use specific reasons and details to support your answer.

Some people believe that success comes from hard work. Others believe that success has to do with luck. Which opinion do you agree with and why? Give specific details and examples to support your opinion.

Some people think the media – television and films – negatively affect people's behaviour. Others do not think so. How do you think the media affects people's behaviour?
Use specific reasons and examples to support your answer.

Some people believe that progress is always good. Others believe in preserving tradition. Which do you think is more important and why? Use specific reasons and examples to support your opinion

Do we have to plan for the future? Or stay focused on our present? What is your opinion and why?
Provide examples to support your stand.

How do advertisements affect the trend of people and economy?
Give specific reasons and examples to support your answer.

Some people believe that only people who have a lot of money are successful. Others believe that success does not always equate to having lots of money. Which statement do you agree with and why? Give specific details and examples in your answer.

In some companies, social skills is given priority over qualifications when screening their possible employees. Discuss the advantages and disadvantages of this situation.
Provide specific reasons and examples to support your opinion.

Countries should restrict foreign companies from opening offices and factories in order to protect local businesses. Do you agree or disagree?
Give reasons and specific examples to explain your answer.

Young people prefer listening to music rather than listening to the news on the radio. Is this a positive or a negative trend?

Provide reasons and examples for your opinion.

Some films are designed to make people think, while other films are designed to entertain or amuse people. Which type of film do you prefer and why?
Use specific reasons and examples to support your answer.

Give reasons for the popularity of reality TV in the recent years.
Explain the effects on society and the social meaning of this trend.

These days people pay more attention to famous film stars than to famous scientists. Why is this happening?
Explain the trend, giving reasons and examples to support your opinion.

Does too much freedom for – today's children give positive results? Why or why not?
Include specific details and examples to support your answer.

Everything needs to be a bit challenging in order to be enjoyable. Do you agree or disagree with this statement?
Give reasons and specific examples to explain your answer.

What is the impact of computer games on the children of today? Is it helping their development or making them worse? Why and why not?
Use specific reasons and examples to support your answer.

Some people spend more and some spend less for wedding parties, birthday parties and other celebrations? Is it a waste of money or a social requirement? Include specific details and examples to support your choice.

In some countries people place more importance on their retirement years because they will have more time to enjoy their lives and will have shed most of their responsibilities. To what extent do you agree or disagree?
Give specific reasons and examples to support your opinion.

Some people forget national holidays and prefer to celebrate their personal holidays more because more people are becoming less appreciative of their love of country.
To what extent do you agree or disagree? Give specific reasons and examples to support your opinion.

Some parents think that the latest technologies (gadgets, computers, etc.) will help in their child's learning development. Others think giving children the latest gadgets will be a distraction in their studies. Which opinion do you agree with and why?
Give specific details and examples in your answer.

Computer games help parents in the care for their children because they keep children occupied. Do you agree or disagree? To what extent do you agree or disagree?
Give specific reasons and examples to support your opinion.

Some countries spend large amounts of money hosting international sports events like the Olympic Games. Instead, this money should be spent to provide information campaigns and infrastructure to encourage more ordinary people to participate in sports. To what extent do you agree or disagree?
Give specific reasons and examples to support your opinion.

Do you think that public cultural and educational institutions should have a fee? Discuss your opinion and provide specific reasons and examples to support your answer.

Every generation of people is different in important ways. How is your generation different from your parents' generation? Include reasons and details in your explanation.

In some countries, it is normal for older people to live on their own rather than with their children What are the advantages and disadvantages of this trend?
Give reasons and specific examples to explain your answer.

In some countries, people live with their parents and siblings until their old age. Do you think there are more advantages or

disadvantages to this behaviour?
Discuss your opinion and provide specific reasons and examples to support your answer.

Have you ever lived away from your parents? Describe your living situation and explain its advantages and disadvantages.
Include specific details and examples to support your choice.

Some people say that advertisements are not good because it encourages us to buy things we don't really need. Others say that advertisements are good because it informs us about new products that can improve our lives. Which viewpoint do you agree with and why?
Include specific details and examples to support your choice.

Some countries implement a national Identification system where all people's information are stored in a central database under state control. This is believed to be harmful to members of society by some.
Do you support or oppose this opinion? Explain your position.

What are the advantages and disadvantages of shopping online? Share your own experience as an example in your answer. Give specific details and examples in your answer.

Many modern shopping centres are now becoming more popular than local market shops. What are the advantages and disadvantages of this consumer behaviour?
Provide specific reasons and examples to support your position.

Some people prefer to live in a traditional house. Others prefer to live in a modern apartment building. Which do you prefer and why? Give specific details and examples in your answer.

In some developing countries, government funds are spent more on repairing buildings than building new ones. Does this help them save more money in the long run?
Provide specific reasons and examples to support your position.

Some believe that it is better for each family to live by themselves rather than share a house with relatives. Do you agree or disagree? Provide specific reasons and examples to support your position.

Some parents allow their teenage children to live independently, away from home. Other parents do not want their teenage children to live far away from them. Which do you think is better and why? Use specific reasons and details to support your answer.

To what extent do you agree or disagree? Ads manipulate your taste and the way you think.
Give specific reasons and examples to support your opinion.

What is your stand about the issue of young children having mobile phones? Is it beneficial or not? Why?
Include specific details and examples to support your choice.

In the past people used more formal and long expressions to communicate with each other. Nowadays, we use fewer words and are more informal. Why is this happening?
Use examples and specific details to explain your answer.

Compared to the past, more people are now trying to learn a foreign language to increase their chances of landing a better job in their native country or to have better opportunities to work abroad.
To what extent do you agree with this point of view?
Give specific reasons and examples to support your opinion.

People equate a good salary with success. Some say that money is not what will make you successful In your own opinion, what will make a person truly successful? Give specific reasons and examples to support your answer.

Money is the best way to motivate people to perform better in the workplace. To what extent do you agree with this statement.
Provide specific reasons and examples to support your answer.

Many children participate in social networks on the internet instead of participating in community activities in their neighbourhood.

What are the advantages and disadvantages of this situation?
Use specific reasons and examples to support your opinion.

Some people prefer to live in a quiet place, such as the countryside. Others prefer to live in a big city. Which place do you prefer to live in and why? Use specific reasons and examples to support your opinion.

People are becoming less interested in community activities. What is causing this behaviour and what will be the result?
Provide explanations and examples to support your answer.
Some people believe that children should be required to learn other languages at a young age because it will be useful for their personal development.
Do you support or oppose this opinion? Explain your position.

Some people believe that children should be obligated to help with household chores as soon as they are able to. Others believe that children should not be forced to do household chores. Which opinion do you agree with and why?
Use specific reasons and details to support your answer.

Due to computers and their busy lifestyle people do not spend as much time with other people. Do you think this is positive or negative?
Provide specific reasons and examples to support your opinion.

Some argue that film and television are a waste of time, because they do not have a direct connection with people's lives.
To what extent do you agree or disagree?

Many children prefer playing interactive games to playing traditional games. Discuss the advantages and disadvantages.
Provide specific reasons and examples to support your opinion.

Nowadays we are more and more a consumer-oriented society. Discuss the advantages and disadvantages of this situation.
Provide specific reasons and examples to support your opinion.

What are the advantages and disadvantages of shopping online? Share your own experience as an example in your answer. Give specific details and examples in your answer.

Violent news stories should not be shown on television and newspapers because they promote violence. To what extent do you agree or disagree?
Provide specific reasons and examples to support your opinion.

Compared to the past, children now spend more time for playing virtual simulation games and participating in online social networks than meeting people in person to socialize. How has this behaviour affected society?
Discuss the reasons and consequences of this behaviour. Provide specific examples to support your answer.

Do children need to be rewarded when they behave properly? Do we need to punish or beat them if they make mistakes? What is your view on this? Give specific reasons and examples to support you answer.

Some people consider big events, such as, weddings, birthdays and overseas travel as the most significant time of their lives. Others consider their present daily life the most significant time in their lives. Which do you consider more important and why?

Do you think it is necessary to spend a lot of money when people celebrate birthdays or is it better to save the money for other purpose?
Provide specific reasons and examples to support your opinion.

In some countries people are happy when they retire and remain very active. In other countries, they are considered too old to enjoy their lives. Which opinion do you hold?
Provide specific reasons and examples to support your answer.

Some people think that analysing and planning is the right way to achieve things, while others believe that a more easy-going approach is better in life.

Discuss your opinion and give examples.

Some believe that youngsters should be friends with older people rather than fear and respect them. Discuss the advantages and disadvantages of each point of view.
Provide specific reasons and examples to support your opinion.

Children should always start studying foreign languages from an early age. To what extent do you agree or disagree?
Use specific reasons and examples to support your position.

Do you think that teenagers should be left to develop naturally or should be directed towards what their parents think is good for them? Discuss the advantages and disadvantages of these methods.
Provide specific reasons and examples to support your opinion.
These days even young people can become rich and famous. Do you think this is good or bad?

Provide specific reasons and examples to support your answer.

In your own opinion, do you think that advertisements are informative? Why or why not?
Give specific reasons and examples to support you answer.

Some believe that there are too many advertisements in the internet, radio and television and that even the contents of shows and news articles become advertisements themselves. To what extent do you agree or disagree to this statement?
Provide suggestions to address the situation. Give specific examples to explain your answer.

Should buildings in cities be expanded without restrictions or should their size be limited to a certain extent? Discuss the advantages and disadvantages of this limitation.
Provide specific reasons and examples to support your opinion.

Young people prefer living in big cities. What will this tendency lead to? Suggest reasons and results of this trend.

Provide specific reasons and examples to support your answer.

In some countries, buildings of historical value are being demolished to give way to modern buildings. Do you think that it is better to preserve the old historical outlook of buildings or it is better to incorporate only new styles of architecture? Discuss the advantages and disadvantages of this situation.
Provide specific reasons and examples to support your opinion.

In some countries, women are given special days leave for their monthly period. Some think that this is a form of discrimination between genders. Do you agree or disagree?
Provide specific reasons and examples to support your position.

More people now work overseas. What are the reasons why people are doing so? Does this trend have more advantages or disadvantages?
Provide specific reasons and examples to support your opinion.

Some companies now use services of freelancers who work online from their homes. What are the advantages and disadvantages of this trend?
Provide specific reasons and examples to support your opinion.

Nowadays many companies use low paid intern ships and student labour to their benefit. Discuss the advantages and disadvantages of this trend.
Provide specific reasons and examples to support your opinion.

The most popular modern media is the internet. Do you think it will replace all other available media of communication?
Provide specific reasons and examples to support your opinion.

Some couples nowadays prefer to maintain a good career rather than having children? What are the advantages and disadvantages of choosing career over family? Give specific reasons and examples to support you answer.

Would you prefer having children earlier or later in life? How will it affect society as a whole? Give reasons and examples to support your answer.

Some people argue that the best way to have work efficiency is for the worker to work for several days and then takes a few days off. To what extent do you agree or disagree with this arrangement? Provide specific reasons and examples to support your opinion.

Some people think that it is better to stick to one job, while others think when they swap jobs they will have a better chance to gain more knowledge and money. Which do you agree with and why? Discuss both sides and provide specific reasons and examples to support your opinion.

Many people think that having lots of money is the best way to guarantee happiness, while others think that it depends on other factors. Compare these two views.
Provide specific reasons and examples to support your position.

Not all workers get to work on the job they are qualified for. Why do you think this is so?
Provide specific reasons and examples to support your opinion.

Some people think that in modern society one needs to focus on their career while leaving personal development and values behind. What do you think is more important?
Provide specific reasons and examples to support your opinion.

More people now buy products that they do - not need because they are persuaded by advertising.
To what extent do you agree or disagree?
Give specific reasons and examples to support your opinion.

Young people believe that they live in a better world than older generations.
To what extent do you agree or disagree?
Give specific reasons and examples to support your opinion.

Some people believe that hard work is vital for success, while others think that education guarantees success more than anything. Which do you agree with?
Use specific reasons and examples to support your position.

People are more aware of fashion nowadays and it continues to be a huge business, with a lot of advertising involved and millions of dollars of being paid to models. Discuss whether this is a good or bad trend.
Provide specific reasons and examples to support your opinion.

According to some people, living in a big city is not as good for families as living in a small town.
To what extent do you agree or disagree?
Give specific reasons and examples to support your opinion.

2471In some cities, child care centres are situated near business establishments and operate before and beyond office hours so parents can leave their children before work and pick them up on their way home. Will this be good for the child's overall development?

Discuss the advantages and disadvantages of this situation.
Provide specific reasons and examples to support your opinion.

GOVERNMENT

Should the government support artists, such as, -musicians, writers, and-painters? Is it economically beneficial or is it just a waste of money? Why or why not?

Every person is essential to the development of a country. Talk about what you think is your role in the development of your country. Use specific reasons and examples in your explanation.

Why do people from developing countries have a more positive outlook on economic growth than people from developed countries? Does economic growth really improve the standard of living? Explain and give specific reasons and details to support your answer.

Countries should restrict foreign companies from opening offices and factories in order to protect local businesses. Do you agree or disagree?

What is the developmental effect of people who prefer to shop in supermarkets to small shops or local markets? How does it affect the local economy? Give specific reasons and examples to support your answer.

Do you agree or disagree that governments should spend money on other things than art even though art helps develop quality in people's life? Use specific reasons and examples to support your position.

Some countries focus on health care and education benefits while others on infrastructure and employment. Which do you think would be more beneficial for the population? Give specific details and examples to support your opinion.

Compare these views. Politicians have the greatest influence on the world. Scientists make the greatest contribution to the world. Which do you agree with? Use specific reasons and examples to support your position.

How can one's government stop or prevent smuggling of illegal drugs from one country to another? Use specific reasons and examples to support your answer.

In your own opinion, how can the government of each country eradicate or lessen the crimes committed by their own people? Use specific reasons and details to support your answer.

Some people think the government should focus on improving the economy of the country. Other people think the government should focus on social services such as health and education programs. Which statement do you agree with? Explain and provide examples to support your opinion.

SPORTS AND PASTIMES

Some people believe that governments should ban dangerous sports even though others claim they should have the freedom to choose a sport to their liking. To what extent do you agree or disagree?
Give specific reasons and examples to support your opinion.

What book or film do you think portrays a country's culture the best? Would you recommend it to a foreign friend who wishes to learn and understand that country? Describe the book or film and explain why you would recommend it. Use specific reasons and details to support your answer.

International sporting events are costly and bring problems to the hosting country. To what extent do you agree or disagree?
Give specific reasons and examples to support your position.

Some say sports facilities are important and they promote healthy lifestyles while others believe they have only a small impact on individuals. What is your opinion? Use specific reasons and examples to support your answer.

A film can portray the culture and traditions of a country. What films have you watched that tell a specific story of a country?
Use specific examples and details to support your response.

Do you think video games and action films promote violence that could be harmful to children? Why or why not?
Give specific details and examples to support your answer.

Write about a certain hobby that has also provided income for people. Use specific reasons and examples to support your answer.

Some people participate in extra-curricular activities such as volunteering in charitable events or joining dance groups to gain more knowledge and experience. Others simply focus on their goals such as academic studies or work. Which do you think helps in improving a person's knowledge and experience? Use specific reasons and details to support your answer.

Some people say that playing games teaches us about life. Others emphasize that only practical experience teaches us valuable lessons about life. Which statement do you agree with and why? Include specific details and examples to support your choice.

Some people think that watching television does not make people smarter. Other people think that watching television can be informative. Which opinion do you agree with and why?
Use specific reasons and details to support your answer.

Some people think it is okay for adults to play computer games. Others think that only children should play computer games. Which opinion do you agree with and why?
Include specific details and examples to support your choice.

Some parents do not allow their children to watch action films and blood sports or play violent video games because it promotes bad behaviour. Others say it does not. Which opinion do you agree with and why?
Give specific examples and details in your explanation.

Do you agree or disagree with the following statement? Sports can bring world peace.
Give specific reasons and examples to support your answer.

Some people go shopping as a form of recreation. It has replaced the other activities that people used to do as hobbies. Is this a positive or negative development? Use specific reasons and examples to support your answer.

Nowadays shopping has replaced many other activities that people choose as their hobby in their free time. What are the reasons for this? Is this a positive or negative development?

Most people prefer popular fun activities rather than visiting museums. Why? Use examples and details in your answer.

12954199R00069

Printed in Great Britain
by Amazon.co.uk, Ltd.,
Marston Gate.